AF349285

"In a prose style that spirals heavenward like a red-tailed hawk riding a thermal, Emmanuel Vaughn-Lee pours forth perceptions that remind us all to renew our bond at a heart-deep level with the guardian holiness that is our glorious living Earth."

—DAVID JAMES DUNCAN, author of *Sun House*, *The Brothers K*, and *The River Why*

"An exigent cry for remembrance and affirmation of the sacred nature of Earth and our raveled relationship with Her. Wary of the dark, extractive side of New Age culture, Vaughan-Lee offers 'a different way,' an adaptable vision 'grounded in the real' that calls for individual commitment and draws on both existing and fresh ways for embodying a spiritual ecology and for reigniting our ancient relationship with the place that is our home. When you are ready, open your eyes. Turn the page."

—FORREST GANDER, Pulitzer Prize–winning poet

"In our time of deep divisions, Emmanuel Vaughan-Lee reminds us that we are all weavers, and love is the thread. In this time of loneliness, he offers the embrace of a bountiful and beautiful world—flowing rivers and maple trees in autumn. In a time of unspeakable cruelty, he offers healing. In a time of deep disappointment in humanity, he offers an urgent vision of our better selves. In this time of endings, he tells a sweeping new story about a future that is both necessary and possible. These are great gifts. I am filled with gratitude."

—KATHLEEN DEAN MOORE, PHD, author of
Great Tide Rising and *Wild Comfort*

"In the face of a planetary crisis so vast and sweeping it dwarfs the biblical, Vaughan-Lee skillfully seeks to transform a potent grief for the Earth into the attentive Sufi practice of awakened love called 'Remembrance.' There's nothing passive here in this urgent call to begin to actively walk and breathe this love—love that looks not for a 'solution' but for agency energized by the fundamental truth that the Earth is no 'other'!"

—SUSAN MURPHY ROSHI, author of
A Fire Runs Through All Things

"A love song to the Beloved who shimmers and dances in every raindrop. A hymn to the joy of breathing. A luminous and companionable guide through the dark forests of the present. A strenuously practical manual for being properly alive. Essential if you're human, and even more essential if you're not."

—CHARLES FOSTER, PHD, author of
The Edges of the World and *Being a Human*

Remembering Earth

EMMANUEL VAUGHAN-LEE

SHAMBHALA

Shambhala Publications, Inc.
2129 13th Street
Boulder, Colorado 80302
www.shambhala.com

Cover art: Bryan Nash Gill, *Cedar Burl*, 2011
Cover & interior design: Kate E. White

9 8 7 6 5 4 3 2 1

First Edition
Printed in the United States of America

Shambhala Publications makes every effort to print on acid-free, recycled paper.
Shambhala Publications is distributed worldwide by Penguin Random House, Inc.,
and its subsidiaries.

LIBRARY OF CONGRESS CATALOGING-IN-PUBLICATION DATA
Names: Vaughan-Lee, Emmanuel author
Title: Remembering earth: a spiritual ecology / Emmanuel Vaughan-Lee.
Description: First edition. | Boulder, Colorado: Shambhala Publications, Inc.,
[2026] | Includes bibliographical references.
Identifiers: LCCN 2025042780 | ISBN 9781645475101 hardback
Subjects: LCSH: Ecology—Religious aspects—Islam | Sufism
Classification: LCC BP190.5.N38 V38 2026
LC record available at https://lccn.loc.gov/2025042780

The authorized representative in the EU for product safety and
compliance is eucomply OÜ, Pärnu mnt 139b-14, 11317 Tallinn,
Estonia, hello@eucompliancepartner.com.

CONTENTS

PART ONE

REMEMBRANCE

INTRODUCTION

I

This book grew out of a series of lectures I gave between fall 2022 and summer 2024 at St. Ethelburga's Centre for Reconciliation and Peace in London and The Sharpham Trust in Devon on the theme of spiritual ecology. These lectures—and in turn, this book—draw from my Sufi tradition, mystical experiences, and practice of embodied spiritual ecology. My work over the past twenty years as a filmmaker, magazine editor, and curator, weaving the threads connecting ecology, culture, and spirituality through the alchemical power of story, has also deeply influenced the themes explored here. While the lectures have been adapted and revised for this medium, I've preserved aspects of their original oral storytelling form that is circular in nature. Repetition is present throughout as I return to central ideas and teachings again and again. This is purposeful, as the subject matter itself is cyclical and the text seeks to evoke this rhythm directly.

The term *spiritual ecology* is relatively new, having been first introduced in the mid-2000s by the scholar Leslie E. Sponsel and quickly taken up by many prominent writers, thinkers, and teachers within the fields of environmentalism, religion, and spirituality. It offered a way to help articulate the spiritual dimension of the ecological crisis, the root causes behind it, and the role of an engaged spirituality as a response. While many consider it to be a further evolution of deep ecology, an environmental philosophy based on the understanding that the environment is a living whole comprised of beings that should all be respected, I feel its roots are much older and are reflected in the depths of Earth-based cultures, Indigenous wisdom, and spiritual and mystical traditions throughout the world.

One of the first writers and teachers to adopt this term was my father, the Sufi master Llewellyn Vaughan-Lee, whose seminal book *Spiritual Ecology: The Cry of the Earth* was hugely influential in seeding this field. This collection of essays edited by my father, from writers and teachers including Thich Nhat Hanh, Wendell Berry, Joanna Macy, and Vandana Shiva, showcased not only the universality of spiritual ecology but also its increased importance as an awareness of climate change, biodiversity loss, and ecological destruction (to name just a few of the many crises we are facing) entered the mainstream collective consciousness. My own work as a filmmaker, and later as the founder of

Emergence Magazine, was significantly shaped by my father's writing and teachings and his emphasis on the need for spiritual and mystical traditions to work more directly with and on behalf of the Earth. It was in part this call that led me to leave behind a career as a jazz musician in my mid-twenties and embark on a very different journey as a documentary filmmaker to tell stories about our relationship with the living world. But my real relationship with spiritual ecology began much earlier.

I was born into a mystical family in London in 1979. My father had met his spiritual teacher, a Russian Sufi mystic named Irina Tweedie, in 1972 when he was nineteen. My mother studied with the renowned mystical British painter Cecil Collins in the mid-seventies and shortly after was introduced to Irina Tweedie and became her student. A few months after I was born my father bought a house on a residential tree-lined street in North London and invited Irina Tweedie to live and teach in the ground-floor flat. I grew up with a guru living downstairs.

Irina Tweedie had traveled to India in the late 1950s in search of spiritual meaning and truth, and there she met a Sufi master named Radha Mohan Lal from the Naqshbandiyya-Mujaddidiyya tradition. She spent the next several years with him before his death in 1966, became his successor, and brought this ancient Sufi lineage to the West. During her time in India she gave away all her money, and upon returning to London lived solely on her war widow's pension in a tiny one-room flat, with the London overground train rattling by outside her window. In her early days as a teacher she had only a small number of students, my parents among them, who would all cram into her flat to sit in her presence, practice silent meditation, and hear stories of her experiences with her teacher.

The invitation to live in our house coincided with the publication of her book *Daughter of Fire*, a deeply personal and detailed account of her spiritual training in India. It became a bit of a spiritual bestseller, attracting seekers from all over the world who were drawn both to her potent presence and the ancient Sufi tradition she had brought from India. Her students quickly grew in number and our house became a kind of a modern ashram, with up to a hundred people coming and going each day. People from all walks of life and every religious background would gather outside the house waiting for the door to open at 2 p.m. Six days a week our home was open—a place for people to come for meditation, prayer, and teachings. Anyone with a sincere desire for God or Truth was welcome: bankers, artists, schoolteachers, carpenters, rock stars—even a policeman who, walking by the street one day and noticing a hundred pairs of shoes outside the doorstep, rang the doorbell to find out what was going on. He ended up staying for six years.

I grew up immersed in these comings and goings, surrounded by spiritual aspirants and those drawn to the Sufi path, but it was the immersion in Divine remembrance and the intoxicating sweetness of love that left a lasting imprint. Sufis are known as lovers of God, drawn to experiencing the Divine through the longing, intoxication, sweetness, and pain of mystical love. The different forms of Sufism, or paths (*tariqas*), have each developed ways of evoking love as a means to transcend the ego and draw one closer to God, who, as it is said in the Qur'ān, is closer to you than your jugular vein (Surah Qaf–50:16). Some use music or dance, as in the famous whirling dervishes of the Mevlevi order, whose founder, Jalāl al-Dīn Muḥammad Rūmī, was the most famous of all the Sufi poets. Others practice a vocal *dhikr*, or mantra, repeating the names of God or various prayers until they enter a trancelike intoxicated state where one experiences the nearness of the Divine. In the Naqshbandiyya-Mujaddidiyya tradition I was born into, this nearness and Divine love is evoked through the practice of a silent dhikr, where one repeats the name of God continuously on the in- and out-breath, and through a heart-based meditation known as *dhyana*, which simply means "meditation" in Sanskrit.

The presence of a teacher and seekers engaged in these practices, and the energy of love they emanated, filled my childhood. My father meditated for hours each day, starting long before dawn, and had learned to be in a constant state of remembrance of God early in his journey, before I was born. At the age of six I began meditating and joining the others downstairs in the afternoon after school. It wasn't because I was told to, or even asked if I would like to join, but rather because I was drawn. I meditated easily and deeply, as children often can, not yet burdened by the weight of the ego and the conditioning of the mind. Learning through spiritual texts is not emphasized in our path, but rather direct experience, service, selflessness, and humility. Still, I was taught certain foundational Sufi precepts and principles, some specific to my own tradition, like the practice of solitude in the crowd (*khalwat dar anjuman*), where one's attention remains inwardly with God while outwardly present in the midst of life, never forgetting God for one instant. Others were more broad and central to all forms of Sufism, such as the Oneness of Being (*waḥdat al-wujūd*), an ontology attributed to the great thirteenth-century Sufi master, poet, and philosopher Ibn ʿArabī, which states simply that everything in existence—from the universe to every distinct being on Earth, including humans—is a manifestation of God.

The understanding of the Oneness of Being was implicit in my upbringing. It was not intellectualized or philosophized, but rather reflected and embodied by Irina Tweedie, my parents, and the other seekers I grew up around. Everything was God. The apple tree at the end of the garden, the fox scurrying across the grass, the clouds, the rain, even the concrete sidewalk lining our street. It simply meant everything was to be respected because everything was divine and interconnected with everything else in existence—easy enough for a child to grasp, and something that made absolute sense to me. That this understanding was not recognized by the majority of people in the culture outside my home was perhaps less clear to me at the time.

The understanding this gave me also meant that experiences of the Divine in one's practice—inner states of stillness, peace, or love—were not elevated above the phenomenal world but recognized as a different and more direct form of God, and that the Creator wasn't better than the creation, but rather creation was a form of the Creator. As it states in the Qur'ān, "Wherever you turn there is the face of God" (Surah Al-Baqarah–2:115). This understanding and foundational teaching infused all aspects of my inner and outer life, and it helped explain other basic teachings: Treat others (including nonhuman beings) with respect and reverence, live simply, walk lightly on the Earth, and don't take more than you need. And perhaps most central of all: Whatever you do, do it with love, for it is love that is at the center of everything.

II

When I was eleven, Irina Tweedie retired, my father became her successor, and soon after we moved from London to Northern California to open a retreat center. We settled in a small town on the coast about an hour and a half north of San Francisco, at the edge of a national park. The house we moved into was nestled deep in the woods with no direct neighbors, overlooked a nearby bay and wetlands, and was just a short drive from the Pacific Ocean. There weren't enough bedrooms in the house, so I moved into an old cabin on the property that had been built by hippies in the sixties in the shape of a ship. It was damp, had mice and bats, a woodstove for heat, and pictures of the Rolling Stones embedded in the redwood-planked wall. It couldn't have been more different from the small, nondescript, white-plastered room looking out on a residential street in London. I loved it.

At the small local school, I experienced severe bullying and struggled to adjust, but I found solace and refuge in the woods, beaches, and expansive ocean. I had always loved nature (as I called it then) as a child, but my experience of it had been limited to parks and gardens in the city, short visits to the countryside, and occasional trips to the Swiss Alps. Here nature was all around me all the time. Instead of people gathering outside our doorstep, grazing deer and the cacophony of birdsong greeted me. I soon began exploring nearby trails, forests, and beaches, most of them usually empty of people. I learned to forage for mushrooms after the autumn rains and swim in the creeks and hidden ponds in the hills during the summer. I started surfing and soon came to love the cold embrace of the wild Pacific and the power of the waves. Entering the water, I would feel immersed in something large, unknown, and constantly shifting. My emotions, troubles at school, and all else would temporarily be absorbed in this great expanse. It felt like meditation.

Oneness of Being, which I had understood and felt through my spiritual practice, became a more visceral experience, more alive and rooted in place. My relationship with the Earth began to feel embodied in a way it hadn't in London. Here nature had a real wild presence, unlike the more subdued and manicured one in English parks and gardens. I found there was a space of emptiness present within this landscape that resonated deeply with me. I would often visit my favorite beach, where I could walk alone for miles along the shore while reading a book. I would look back and see my footprints alongside the shoreline, as if two worlds were weaving in and out. I didn't have a name for it then, but looking back, it's clear that a relationship with the Earth was taking root that reflected my inner experiences of love, silence, and the Divine.

When I was fifteen I fell completely in love with jazz and improvisation, eventually dropping out of high school so I could devote myself more fully to music. At the same time this new love was emerging, a more formal spiritual training, as my father called it, began. My life, outwardly through music and inwardly through meditation and dhikr, became very much grounded in practice. I spent many hours each day with my instrument in my hands, while also making space for silence and love in my heart and the constant remembrance of God. This emphasis continued over the next ten years as my journey with improvised music grew into a career and my inner life deepened and in turn became more experiential. And while my relationship with the living world wasn't always as consciously present during these years, especially when studying music at university in Boston, it was always there in the background.

When I was twenty-five something shifted and I found myself increasingly unsettled. Despite a blossoming music career, I felt called to leave it behind and seek a way to engage more directly in outer life with what had been pulling at me inwardly. I was becoming more and more concerned by how mainstream culture was ignoring the signs of a world falling out of balance. Global warming (as it was called then) barely seemed a consideration, the post-9/11 wars were running rampant in Iraq and Afghanistan, and materialism and consumerism continued to grow unabated. These imbalances evoked something deep inside me, what I now recognize as an ancestral or spiritual memory—a felt sense of a once-sacred relationship with the Earth that was being broken or violated. I wanted to find a way to explore and express more directly what I had experienced inwardly in my practice and in my relationship with the living world.

During this time I became very interested in the power of documentary film as a medium, one that allowed me a more direct form of storytelling than music and was capable of engaging the issues, ideas, and values I was drawn to explore. At the core of my interest in filmmaking were two central questions: What is the relationship between spirituality and the world at this moment in time? And what role does spiritual wisdom, ontologies like the Oneness of Being, spiritual practice, and the universal spiritual values that have emerged over millennia in so many traditions play in a world that is coming apart at the seams?

Before long I was traveling the world interviewing people and making documentaries. At first, I naively cast my net rather wide, exploring this question broadly (and holistically, I thought), looking at how it related to social and cultural issues, politics, economics, spirituality, religion, and the environment. But soon my focus narrowed to our relationship with the living world, in part because, again and again, my query across these diverse fields would often lead back to the Earth and to the realization that our spiritual disconnection from Her is at the root of the myriad crises we are facing.

Over the next fifteen years I made many environmental films, often at the edges of the world where climate change and ecological destruction were being felt most acutely. Each told a story of different people, a different place, and a different way the dominant culture is contributing to the destruction of the living world. But at the heart of each film were two basic questions, two parts of a single story: What happens when spirit becomes disconnected from matter? How can it become connected again?

These are the questions I've been asking over and over: asking others, asking myself, and over time learning more and more to ask the Earth Herself. I began doing this through films, then over the past decade through *Emergence Magazine*, which since its inception has focused directly on exploring and expanding the field of spiritual ecology. As the years have gone by and more stories have been told and shared, I feel more strongly than ever that stories are alive, that they are alchemical vessels of transformation that hold space for creation and renewal, that they can play a vital role in helping to heal the divide between spirit and matter, and that the good ones have the potential to teach us how to love the Earth again.

The story I share in this book is the central thread that emerged at the confluence of my Sufi tradition, twenty years of posing these questions, and ultimately listening to the voice of the Earth Herself. It is at its core a journey of remembrance—a return to the sacred nature of creation.

III

Part two of the book includes practices that I have taught within my Sufi tariqa, which in recent years has recognized the need, within its traditional framework, for a direct spiritual relationship with the Earth. The practices focus on what is simplest and most fundamental: the breath, the heart, walking, listening, time, and prayer. While they are inspired by the practices and teachings rooted in my own Sufi tariqa, they are universal in nature. Each one is an invitation to awaken what is most ancient within us and to embrace a spiritual ecology.

Throughout the book I refer to the Divine as God, Truth, and, most of all, the Beloved—these are just some of the many names that the all-encompassing mystery has come to be called. I refer to the Divine as They/Them rather than the traditional He/Him, for as the majority of the world's great traditions tells us, God is both masculine and feminine, as well as beyond any gender classification and completely unknowable. God has never felt like a distinct He or She to me, but as both, and also very much beyond gender, so naming the Divine as nonbinary is more authentic to my experience.

The Earth, however, is most certainly a She, and I refer to Her as such. She is the great life-giving divine being and creative force known by many names: Gaia, Pachamama, Prithvi, Bhumi Devi, Sophia, and of course Mother Earth, to name but a few. It is to Her earthly embrace that we are being invited to return, to Her voice that we must listen once more, Her ceaseless giving that we must again come to respect, and the ancient memory of our relationship with Her that we must awaken.

A Primordial Covenant of Relationship

In the early days of the COVID-19 pandemic in 2020, the world was thrust into a shared experience of vulnerability and disorientation. The familiar ground beneath us shifted and the future became unknowable. More than simply disrupting daily life, the pandemic dismantled our illusions of stability, exposing deep fractures within the systems we rely on. What had once appeared as minor cracks were laid bare as gaping chasms, revealing not only the fragility but also the falsity of the world we had constructed.

As we remained locked down in our homes watching our world unravel, it was hard to ignore the weight of the moment. Millions of lives were being lost to the virus, while further ruptures began dismantling life in other ways. What had long been a reality for many—a life lived on the edge of crisis, shaped by the fateful consequences of colonization, imperialism, capitalism, and greed—suddenly became a collective reckoning. The killing of George Floyd, an African American man violently asphyxiated by a white police officer during a routine arrest, ignited a wave of resistance that rippled far beyond the borders of the United States as people came together to demand an end to systemic oppression and racism. Soon after, war erupted in Ukraine, sending shock waves of violence and displacement across Europe and upending the post–World War II sense of security in the region. And in Iran the brutal killing of Mahsa Amini, a young woman taken into custody and severely beaten by Iran's religious morality police for not wearing a hijab, sparked a powerful movement as women took to the streets under the rallying cry: *Woman, Life, Freedom.* Amid fear and uncertainty, a rising tide of authoritarianism and right-wing politics began to take hold across the United States and Europe, manifesting as nationalism, repression, and the steady erosion of rights.

As these upheavals unfolded, the Earth Herself mirrored the unrest: Wildfires raged throughout California, Australia, the Amazon, and the Congo Basin; floods submerged entire villages in Pakistan; and record-shattering heat waves were experienced across continents, 2023 becoming the hottest year on record, only to be surpassed in 2024. These were not isolated disasters, but a glimpse of a wider collapse.

This convergence of crises—global sickness, social uprising, ecological destruction—was unrelenting. Where

I live, it had already become routine each autumn to wear N95 masks to shield against the smoke from wildfires burning through forests and towns across Northern California. But in the fall of 2020, the flames came to my doorstep. A ferocious lightning storm, unlike anything we'd ever seen before, ignited fires along the whole West Coast from California to Washington state. For over two months, the blaze consumed everything in its path, transforming familiar landscapes into ash and smoke. The death of trees, animals, and entire ecosystems was no longer abstract but had arrived as a visceral presence, falling as gray remains around me.

Navigating the unknown has always been part of the human story, and yet this moment of change is unfolding within an unprecedented global polycrisis of overlapping and interdependent issues that is vaster in scale than anything we have experienced before. While the challenges we're facing are overwhelming, they are most likely just a foretaste of what lies ahead in the decades to come. In a hundred years we may look back at this time as the calm before the storm, a moment that preceded a world increasingly destabilized and ravaged by conflict, climate change, social upheaval. Yet any story of transformation, both personal and collective, is born from the crucible of crisis, inviting us to imagine how we might reorient ourselves in an uncharted time.

The experience of the pandemic was, in many ways, a global initiation: a threshold moment where the veils were lifted, revealing what had long been obscured. In times of initiation, whether personal or collective, there is always the potential for transformation. Things can shift, old attachments and illusions can fall away, and what is nonessential burns in the fire of change. Initiation is a burning—not a burning of destruction alone, but of renewal. It clears the path for what truly matters to emerge.

Initiation always requires that you walk in a field of ashes, confronting what has been lost, just as I did outside my home. And within this space where much is burned away, in the starkness of what remains there is an invitation to return to what is real; in the process of return something essential is revealed. During the pandemic we all experienced the revelation of what truly matters—kindness, compassion, care for one another, and the shared breath that connects all life. These revelations, stripped of pretense, point to what endures. And from this place of what is real and essential, new futures can take root and begin to grow.

How do we find and begin to work with those roots that will hold us steadfast through the unraveling of our world? What pathways of healing can we walk in such a time? And how do we bear witness to profound loss and the grief that follows without becoming consumed, so that we remain present and able to participate in what is still unfolding? To respond to these questions, we need to look beyond the immediate experience of living with the unknown. We must situate them within the larger story that has given rise to this moment, one that is not new but ancient. It is the story of our time: a story of forgetfulness.

This story of forgetfulness has held the world in its grip for centuries. My friend the late eco-Buddhist philosopher Joanna Macy called it "The Great Unraveling"—a collapse of all that has been built on illusion, like a house of cards falling away.[1] At its heart lies a great forgetting of creation's sacred nature. This forgetfulness has fractured the fundamental relationship between human beings and the living Earth, separating what was once whole. It has led to a crisis of separation, tearing apart the human and the more-than-human world and pushing the sacred, once woven through all of life, to the margins of memory. The climate crisis, for all its urgency, is not at its core a crisis of emissions or even of capitalism and greed. These are symptoms, expressions of a deeper rupture: the loss of an ancient connection, a sacred kinship that has bound us to the Earth since time immemorial.

And yet within this story of forgetfulness lies the possibility of remembrance. Joanna called this "The Great Turning"—a turning toward the sacred, a return to what was forgotten. This story is not without pain, for remembrance often requires us to confront the depths of our forgetfulness and the consequences it has wrought. But through that pain, by walking through the ashes, we are invited back to what it means to be human in the most essential sense, back to connection, kinship, reciprocity, and relationship with the living Earth and all its beings. Within this story lies the potential for transformation, for healing, and for the restoration of a sacred bond that has always been ours to hold.

How do we find our ground in a groundless reality where the world can shift in an instant? First we must recognize that the ground we stood on was never real. It was built on illusion, on quicksand and falsehoods. Then we turn away from the illusion. This means recognizing how we have ignored the sacred nature of creation and approaching creation once more with respect and, ultimately, with love.

Because this is a story of love. It is as much a story of love as it is a story of forgetfulness and remembrance. At the heart of that primordial relationship between humanity and Earth is love—not fleeting or sentimental, nor even solely human, but a love that is vaster, simpler, more ancient. It is a covenant of love between the human and the living Earth, a binding force understood by ancient cultures since the beginning.

These cultures wove this love into the fabric of their existence. Their ceremonies, songs, prayers, and dances were expressions of this love, its language made visible. It was their foundation, their remembrance, and their offering. This love was not passive or indulgent but active and reciprocal, inspiring awe and respect. It demanded humility before the majesty of creation: the storm, the tidal wave, the unknowable mysteries of the living world. This was not fear in the sense of terror, but reverence, a deep respect for the mystery, for what cannot be fully understood.

Now, as we find ourselves in a time of the unknown, we are being called back to reverence. To navigate this space we must return to something that can hold us in the midst of uncertainty. The sacred nature of creation can hold us, but it must be more than an abstract idea. Love for the sacred is not a concept; it is something we feel in the heart, the gut, the body. It is more real than the pavement beneath our feet. It carries substance and depth, layers of history, and a web of relationships woven through time.

We have forgotten this, but that does not mean it is lost. We are not tasked with creating something new. Instead, we are called to return to what already exists. Even if it lies dormant, buried deep within us, it remains. It is in our bones, in our DNA, in the marrow of who we are. And it waits patiently, endlessly, to be remembered.

This love is forgiving of our forgetfulness because it wants to be awoken, it wants to be reclaimed and lived in right relationship. For much of our history we lived in a state of remembrance with this love at the root of our entwinement with Earth. Our past reaches far deeper than we imagine, stretching into epochs when this covenant of love guided our existence.

Moments of great turmoil, initiations such as the one we are living through and those that will most certainly come in the future, can wake us. This global initiation concerns more than a virus, more than social upheaval and war, more than a changing climate and the rise of the authoritarian political right. It is part of a larger story that has been illuminated by all this chaos—the story of connection, of how closely we live, of how deeply intertwined we are. It has revealed the fragility of what we thought was unshakable: Our society is built on illusion, and it is a house of cards with no foundation.

Suffering has the power to break us open. And in that breaking something long dormant can stir. The heart, so often overlooked as a vehicle of transformation, begins to awaken. It feels, remembers, and leads us back to our deepest selves. There is great power in being thrown back on ourselves, in rediscovering what it means to feel love. If we are to move forward from this crisis—this crisis within a crisis within a crisis—the path ahead must be built on a foundation of what is real. And nothing is more real than love.

At its core this is a spiritual crisis, and any true response must be a spiritual response. This does not mean that we should neglect practical action. We must do our best to reduce pollution and emissions, to simplify our lives so that we are no longer reckless consumers, and to seek real-world solutions to the crises we face. But these solutions, no matter how well-intentioned, will remain hollow if they are not grounded in love for the Earth. Without love, we ignore the heart of the crisis: the deeper spiritual rupture. And in doing so, we also miss the lesson we might learn and the contribution we are being called to make.

Suffering, loss, and grief can open our hearts. From that openness we can begin to live and act from a place of love and remembrance of the sacred nature of creation. This shift is not only transformative; it also offers us a grounding that remains even when the literal or metaphorical ground beneath us is taken away. The love that binds humanity and the living Earth is not governed by human rules, nor is it ours to control. It is part of that ancient, primordial covenant of relationship, greater than any individual yet intimate enough to hold, nourish, and sustain us. It is real.

But this relationship, like all relationships, demands our effort. It demands attention and care. It asks for our engagement, for our own ways of remembering, honoring, and participating in it. This is not a passive bond. It is alive, dynamic, and reciprocal. And while it may seem daunting, there is comfort in knowing that none of this is new. Nothing we are being asked to do is new. It may take a different form in a different time, but the essence remains the same. The prayers, ceremonies, dances, songs, and poems of our ancestors are technologies of love and remembrance, threads braided between the human and the living Earth.

With each breath, each step, each syllable of those ancient songs, love and remembrance are strengthened. And while times and contexts have changed, we can still return to these practices, albeit in different forms. They need not be elaborate. It can be as simple as holding a moment of silence each morning, recognizing the sacred nature of the living Earth in your heart before stepping outside. It can be walking, consciously acknowledging with each step that you are in relationship with the Earth beneath your feet. It can be breathing, recognizing that every inhale and exhale is an act of communion, not isolation, and honoring that relationship with intention.

These simple practices are rooted in the ways humanity has moved, breathed, and lived on this Earth. The breath has been the foundation for sacred practice in traditions across the world for time beyond measure. Walking in a sacred manner, too, has always been an act of connection. For eons we navigated landscapes and traversed great distances across the surface of the Earth on foot, the soles of our feet always in contact with Her skin. These ways of being are not innovations; they are remembrances of what has always been.

Yes, there were ceremonies, festivals, and special prayers to mark the sacred rhythms of life, to honor deities and ancestors and holy days. These moments were and are vital. But even between the days of celebration, in the quiet rhythm of everyday life, there was a constant remembrance of creation's sacred nature. It was so fundamental that it needed no explanation, no justification. It simply was. Now, in this time of unraveling, we are invited to return to that simplicity, to remember what has been forgotten. To weave once again the threads of love and remembrance into the fabric of our days. It is not a task of invention, but of reconnection; it is an act of humility, reverence, and belonging.

This remembrance is in the marrow of who we are; it is a cry waiting to be heard. It doesn't require us to have university degrees or attend retreats or weekend workshops. It only asks for our attention, openness, and, above all, love. With love, this remembrance settles deep within us. And from this a transformation occurs. We begin to see differently, feel differently, and hear differently. The world ceases to be a backdrop to our lives, and we realize that *we* are the backdrop to Her story.

This is another aspect that remembrance reveals: the journey of listening. To truly listen—to hear the winds as voices, to understand the call of a bird, to feel the rain not as weather but as communion—we must first be grounded in a real connection with the living Earth. Listening is not passive. It requires a willingness to be opened by heartbreak, by pain, by suffering. Only then can we hear the languages of the Earth—the voices of the world that have always been speaking to us. Only then can we hear the stories that are waiting to be told and return to what the geologian Thomas Berry called "the great conversation."[2]

Listening is essential for whatever lies ahead. Whatever emerges from the ashes of this time must be born of listening, not imposition. We have imposed ourselves for too long. But when we approach from a place of love and remembrance, the Earth Herself begins to speak. Voices and stories rise like sprouts from the ground, waiting to be seen, heard, and nurtured. These stories and the voices they carry are pathways to healing; they are ways to find ground in a groundless reality.

But we must also hold the loss. To live in this time is to bear witness to immense grief. We cannot turn away from it. With a foundation of remembrance, we can hold this grief without being consumed by it. We become a container, grounded and steady, capable of bearing both the sorrow of forgetfulness and the hope of awakening. For we are living in a world of unraveling, yes, but also in a world that can awaken. Grounded in remembrance, love, and reverence for the sacred, we can face the enormity of what is unfolding.

We do not know the future—how high the seas will rise, how many forests will burn, how many songs and voices of creatures will fall silent. We do not know. But we know this: Things have been set in motion that cannot be undone. If we believe we can control what is coming, our hubris knows no bounds. Instead, we must return to and live what is essential. We must bear witness to the losses yet to come—losses even greater and harder than we can imagine—while also looking toward a future built on love, remembrance, and the sacred. These must be our foundation, guiding us in the ways we live, listen, and create.

TWO

Stepping into the Liminal

We are living in a liminal time. The liminal is a space between worlds, a threshold to be crossed as one world comes to an end and another begins, delicate and nascent. This in-between space is more than a moment of transition; it is an invitation. It draws us into the unknown, into a place where the familiar dissolves and the landscapes of our existence begin to shift.

The liminal is not merely theoretical. In the wake of seismic shifts like the pandemic, structures that once appeared unshakable are revealed as fragile and unsustainable, even unreal. So much is laid bare. If we look closely, if we peer between the cracks, we begin to see that the world we have known is not as sturdy as it once seemed. In these times, a space opens between the old world and the new and asks something of us. It challenges us to find our bearings, but it also invites us to step into a new way of being. It is both disorienting and full of possibility.

To enter this space fully, we need to do more than adapt; we must offer ourselves and step into relationship with something greater than ourselves. This space between the worlds allows for a deeper engagement, by necessity perhaps, but also by design. For those paying attention, it demands recognition. It asks us to see the shifting landscape, to acknowledge the unknown, and to notice that the rules we once lived by no longer apply. The old ways of normalcy and a traditional relationship between cause and effect have unraveled; what was reliable is no longer so. We find ourselves in a place where truth is malleable, where the ground beneath our feet feels unsteady and the contours of the future remain undefined.

The first step in navigating this space is acknowledgment—to truly recognize that we are in the liminal, to see clearly that we are living in a time when something is ending. This requires a reckoning, a willingness to take stock of what is real and what is not. On the surface it may appear as though life continues uninterrupted—the trains are full, the motorways are crowded, our phones buzz incessantly with reminders of a world that we are expected to fully give ourselves to. But beneath the surface something has shifted irrevocably. The old world has come to an end, even if it still lingers in form. It is no longer alive in the way it once was.

This recognition is essential. Without it, we risk remaining trapped in the illusions and patterns of the past, unable to step fully into the new. We cannot straddle both worlds, one foot in the familiar, the other in the unknown. To enter the liminal we need to consciously release our grip on what was. The patterns of control, domination, and manipulation that defined the old era cannot come with us. Only by letting go can we free ourselves. Without this release, we carry those patterns with us into the new form, burdening the promise of transformation with the weight of the past.

The liminal offers freedom, but only if we are willing to surrender to its uncertainties. To step into the space between worlds we must leave behind the world as we have known it: not in a purely outward sense, as though quitting our jobs or abandoning the world crumbling around us would be the answer, tempting as that might seem; instead, this is a deeper departure, a shift of story, a shift of frame, a shift of understanding. It is an internal reckoning.

Truthfully, we may still need to participate in the old world to some degree. Few of us can vanish into the wilderness to live entirely off-grid, but this limitation does not mean we need to give ourselves over to the illusion of the past. We can acknowledge it for what it truly is: a mirage, a dream that has held us captive for far too long. And in that acknowledgment we are faced with a choice: to fully wake up and step into a new space or to remain semi-asleep, avoiding the responsibility of seeing what is unfolding.

To wake is to free ourselves—if not physically, then in our minds, our hearts, and our consciousness—from the grasp of what has been. It is to create a necessary space of separation, a pause in which we can begin to see our relationship with the Earth in a new light. From this place of freedom, however tenuous, we gain a new perspective. Where once we were entangled, unable to see beyond the immediacy of our circumstances, there is now room to witness. With distance our vision expands. We can look back at what has unfolded and begin to perceive what is happening in the present. We are no longer reactive, no longer caught in the grip of old patterns. From this place of spaciousness, understanding deepens and the world appears differently.

To witness is not merely to observe; it is to see with clarity and presence, to hold what is before us without turning away. And there is so much that demands our witnessing at this time. The shifts we are living through are monumental, mythic in scale. When the ice caps melt, the seas rise, the forests burn, and entire species vanish, we are no longer in the realm of the ordinary. Only the language of myth can encompass the magnitude of what is unfolding. It is a story so vast, so sweeping, that it dwarfs the biblical. And we are living within it.

To witness is to take responsibility. We must witness what is unfolding—both intimately, in the landscapes of our own lives, and collectively, in the greater, shared experience of these shifting times. We cannot bypass the darkness or ignore the unraveling that demands our attention. Any true transformation, whether within ourselves or the wider world, requires us to turn toward the darkness because within it lies the light.

The world is calling us to witness. Both the living world and the human world are crying out for our acknowledgment. But this act of witnessing requires balance: to give our attention without becoming consumed by fear or immobilized by despair. It is to observe with clarity, to acknowledge with presence, and to remain grounded enough to respond. This is the power of stepping into the liminal, into the space between worlds. From this vantage point, we bear witness without being caught in the entanglements of the old patterns and dynamics. It is as though we have stepped outside the house we have been living in and finally see that its roof is caving in, the walls rotted. This simple yet profound act of stepping back allows us to perceive the unfolding of events in a new light.

Witnessing operates on many levels. On a collective level it means holding space for the distant shifts we hear about daily and what we have come to call climate change and biodiversity loss—the melting ice, the burning forests, the disappearing species. This witnessing carries immense power when approached with maturity and presence. It asks us to say, *I see you. I acknowledge what is happening.*

But it also asks us not to be overtaken, caught in the grip of eco-anxiety. Because if we are caught, we are not free. And if we are not free, we cannot be of service to this moment.

To witness is to let our hearts break open. And if our hearts do not break, we need to go back and look again. What is unfolding demands a response from the heart. It demands that we feel the grief, the pain, the cry of the Earth. This grief is not a weakness; it is a key. It unlocks something essential within us. It is an honest and true response.

If we are to remember the Earth as a sacred, living being, then our response must reflect that truth. If the Earth is dying, or sick, or in pain, and we cannot respond with grief, with sorrow, with a sense of profound loss, then our response is not authentic. It is not honest. Just as we would grieve for a loved one in pain, so too should we grieve for the Earth. To feel deeply is to affirm the sacredness of what we are witnessing. It is to honor the living world not as an abstract concept but as a being that we are in relationship with, one that asks for our presence, our attention, and our hearts.

There are always truths that are revealed in times of crisis, calling to us through the fractures and unraveling of the world we have known. If we witness these truths from the right place within ourselves—with the space and clarity that stepping into the liminal provides—it has the power to unlock something deep within us. Truth, when encountered fully, strikes us in a way that nothing else can. It resonates at our core. And when we are present with it, when we bear witness with attention and openness, something shifts. A doorway opens. And often what pours out is grief.

Many of us have already felt this grief. If we are awake and paying attention, how could we not feel grief when confronted with the suffering of the living world, its beautiful beings in pain? But grief is not a singular event. It is not something to be checked off a list, as though one could say, *I have grieved, and now I am done.* Grief is cyclical, continuous. To be truly awake to this moment is to walk with grief as a constant companion.

When held with consciousness, grief has the power to transform us. Just as stepping away from the illusions of the old world requires us to recognize them, holding grief requires awareness. It requires saying, *This is real. This is overwhelming. But this is not something to run from.* When we do this, grief becomes a series of doorways, each leading deeper into ourselves. First, we turn away from the world we have known and say, *No, not this.* A doorway opens. Then, as we witness the unraveling, another doorway appears, leading us into grief. And when we hold that grief with consciousness, yet another doorway opens—this time into love.

This is the journey unfolding as one world ends and another begins. It is a painful lesson, but it is also a profound reminder of who we really are. The grief we feel, when we sit with it, reveals a truth: It is not a response to something separate from ourselves. It is shared grief, shared pain, because there is no separate "other." It includes us. This is the lesson we are learning, the truth we are remembering. The Earth is not apart from us; She is our mother, our brother, our sister. The living world is not external to us. She is us.

This knowledge that we are one with the Earth and all Her beings does not need to be taught. We carry the memory of it deep within us. But it is buried so deeply that only something potent, something monumental, can reach it. The grief we feel during these early decades of the twenty-first century has that potency, reflecting the magnitude and mythic nature of what is unfolding. The melting ice, the burning forests, the vanishing species, the displacement of populations—these events are not simply tragic, they are reshaping the story and history of the world. This mythic grief cuts to the core of our being. It shakes us awake, returning us to an ancient memory of what once was.

At the center of that memory is love. Not a Hallmark love or a love defined by human limitations, but an ancient, primordial love. A covenant of relationship between humanity and the living Earth. It is the love that has always been there, waiting to be remembered, waiting to guide us as we step into the new world being born. When that ancient love is awakened, something fundamental shifts. We begin to spin differently, to vibrate on a frequency that has been silent for so long. A note that was buried comes alive, and with it a whole way of being emerges. To feel this love, to let it envelop us, requires courage. It means not running from the grief that opens us to it, nor from the love itself, which can feel equally overwhelming. But when we allow ourselves to remain present, to feel this ancient memory returning, we are held. We are held by something vast, something timeless, something that reminds us of a truth we have always known: There is no other. We are one. The Earth and all the beings are part of us, as we are part of them.

This ancient truth, that we are interconnected in the deepest, most primordial way, is at the core of what we must remember as we step into the emerging world. We are not leaving behind everything that has come before. We are returning to what we have forgotten and beginning again with that foundation. We are leaving behind the era of forgetfulness and moving toward an era of remembrance where the ties of kinship that unite us will guide how we live, how we grow our societies, and the stories we tell. Kinship grows from love. Together they form a foundation of relationship, shaping a new way of being.

Grief has the power to lead us to this love. Anyone who has sat by the bedside of a dying parent or friend knows this intimately. Grief has the ability to crack us open, to make us feel a love we never thought possible, a love that holds sadness, pain, joy, and so much more all at once. This is the potential of grief. It breaks us open, awakening something profound. But the awakening is only the beginning. When this love is stirred, it calls for our responsibility.

Love, once awakened, must be tended. Without attention, it can slip back into forgetfulness, buried again by the patterns, both personal and collective, that have kept it hidden for so long. Witnessing grief requires courage, so too does caring for love. As doors open, each unlocked by grief or truth, they invite us into deeper layers of responsibility. These layers ask for our participation in meaningful, deliberate ways of being.

Anyone who has ever been in love understands this truth. Love, to grow, must be nourished. For love to deepen and evolve into friendship, companionship, or the rich dynamics of a lasting relationship, it requires our attention. Without care love fades; its passion dissipates. To integrate this awakened love into our lives we must attend to it. We must acknowledge it. We must weave it into the fabric of our being, allowing it to shape how we live, how we see the world, and how we relate to all that is around us.

This love is not just a feeling within us. It is a conduit of relationship, an invitation that reaches beyond ourselves. Like tendrils extending outward, love invites the other in. And this love, this *Love* with a capital *L*, is not confined to our hearts alone. It is not ours to contain. It exists both within and beyond us in the greater Heart of the world. When our heart touches that greater Heart, we are changed.

To live in this state of awakened love we must remain attentive. We must nurture it, honor it, and give it what it needs. Because this love is not only what connects us, it is what sustains us. When this ancient love awakens within us it changes everything. It infuses the way we act, the way we live, the way we simply *are*. Wherever we go, whatever we do, this love becomes our constant companion. We walk with love. We breathe with love. We eat with love. We see with love.

Remarkably, this love does not require a life of mysticism or spiritual devotion to find. It is not reserved for the few. The extremity of our time—the intensity of grief and transformation—has unlocked a realm of possibility that once took a lifetime of practice and prayer to reach or that was held by cultures who understood this secret. The grief we carry is so potent that it has opened a doorway to an ancient secret: There is no *other*.

This is the story of our time: to find ways to live with this love at the center, to bring it into every aspect of our being. In this liminal time, where great darkness and great light coexist, we are asked to hold both with open eyes and open hearts. To step away from the familiar, to embrace the discomfort of the unknown, and to meet ourselves fully, even if that means leaving behind old versions of ourselves.

It is not about sustainability or green economies, while those things may happen. It is about something far greater and far simpler: a return to what is real, what is ancient, what is already within us. We do not need to discover it. We need to remember it.

This remembrance is not theoretical or abstract. It is lived, embodied, and experienced. It begins with simple acts of attention—learning the power of silence, the grounding of breath, the humility of being present. These practices return us to who we truly are and remind us that we are not strangers to this world but part of its intricate web, bound by love and kinship to all living things.

So welcome the liminal and the unknown. Welcome this space with open arms. Step into it unafraid, even if it makes you uncomfortable. Recognize that what we contribute to this moment matters, not because of outward action alone but because of the inner truth that grounds it. If the outer is not rooted in the inner, it will fade. Just as love fades without attention, acknowledgment, and care, so too does anything we build when we don't anchor it in an inner truth.

Offering a testament to the connection between love, acknowledgment, and the rhythms of the Earth, the poet N. Scott Momaday writes in *Earth Keeper*:

When we dance the earth trembles. When our steps fall on the earth we feel the shudder of life beneath us, and the earth feels the beating of our hearts, and we become one with the earth. We shall not sever ourselves from the earth. We must chant our being, and we must dance in time with the rhythms of the earth. We must keep the earth.[3]

In these words lies a call to remembrance, to reciprocity. When we give our love, it is not lost in the void but is felt, and there is a response. When we walk and acknowledge the Earth, the Earth acknowledges us in return. A great conversation begins. There is a call and there is a response.

This is the rhythm we are invited to return to. Whether through song or silence, movement or stillness, we are called to chant our being and dance in time with the rhythms of the Earth, to acknowledge, to remember, to return—again and again—to the core of who we are. This is where we are united with all that exists. This is where love begins.

THREE

A Spiritual Ecology

The mystics say we are like seeds, each of us carrying the blueprint for our highest potential that is waiting to unfold. Across diverse traditions, much of the spiritual practices are about unlocking this potential. But a seed holds more than just possibility; it carries memories of its origins, its evolution, its relationships. It has songs, ceremonies, and stories embedded within it. We too hold memories—not only of this life and incarnation but of our species as a whole: where we have come from, how we have evolved. Though the term *spiritual ecology* is often spoken of as a field, a philosophy, or a form, to me at its root it is a memory. Deep within us there is the memory of a time when we lived in relationship with this great Earth, when we recognized Her as an animate, sacred, divine being of which we were a part. This remains true, but it has largely been obscured as our world has shifted from a space of kinship, relationship, and reciprocity to one that sees the great Earth as separate and inert, as a resource to be used. This is not a memory erased but a memory veiled and hidden from us—some memories more than others.

Spiritual ecology is, at its core, achingly simple. It is the recognition of the universal spirit that imbues all living things—a recognition that must be embodied through conscious spiritual engagement with the Earth. It is not about learning something new but remembering something very, very old. Spiritual ecology is as old as humanity itself. Like our common ancestry with all living beings that stems from the single-cell organisms we evolved from, spiritual ecology was there from the beginning of our human story. It *is* our beginning. Our earliest forms of worship and praise recognized and revered the spirit present in the living world. In that time of old, we shared a spiritual connection with the Earth. Our spirit met Her spirit. We shared the same spirit. This felt connection predates religions and what we call the growth of civilization. But slowly it was veiled, covered over, severed by our forgetfulness of who She is by faith-based systems that erased or minimized Her, by ideologies like patriarchy, colonization, capitalism, fascism, militarism, and all the vehicles of our modern era that have torn the fabric of life apart. At its core this is a spiritual crisis that we are being forced to acknowledge. And at the root of this crisis lies a memory still held within us. A memory of a space that we share with this divine, sacred being that is the Earth.

This memory must be awakened. It must come alive in us. Many have already felt it stirring, rising to the surface when we find ourselves in places where She is reflected most strongly: where the noise of human drama is quieted, where the grandeur of Her beauty washes over us like a wave, where we cannot ignore how She offers Herself again and again and again. In those moments we feel this connection. We may even feel love, not as something fleeting but as something woven into the marrow of our bones. Love is as much a part of our physical bodies as it is a part of our spiritual being. Like the breath we share with trees and plants as we exchange carbon dioxide and oxygen, it reveals the coexistence at the heart of our mutual belonging. In these moments of Her grace, of Her beauty, She reveals the ancient truth that has always been at the core of who we are.

But this memory can also be woken up through pain, through grief, through the violence and destruction unfolding all around us—pain that is too immense to ignore. It envelops us, seeps into our world and into our lives. And if we allow it to penetrate us, it touches something deep within—that same memory, that same connection. It stirs the question that is crying out from the center of our being: *Why are we doing this?* There is an ancient love, a love as primal as a child's love for its mother. When this love is awakened, it brings that memory to the surface; it shakes us to the very marrow.

And just as this memory can come alive within us, it can also, so easily, be buried again, sinking back beneath the surface. Our culture offers little reflection of this ancient love and is drowning in distractions, desires, and humancentric ways of being that make it hard to keep our heads above water. And so we ask: *How do we prevent that from happening? How do we allow this awakening to be more than a fleeting moment, to become a lived experience, a way of being, so that it is not lost, so that we do not have to struggle again and again to surface what has already been revealed?*

When we allow ourselves to be changed—through witnessing Her beauty and the grace of Her being, the pain She endures, the grief, the suffering, the destruction we inflict upon Her each day—when we allow ourselves to feel fully, then we can return to that fundamental ancient truth. Not as a philosophy, not as a set of principles or values, but as something that we taste, touch, smell, and feel in all the pores of our body, as an embodiment permeating us from the inside out.

Here again I turn to something ancient to sustain and nurture the awakening of this deep memory. The Sufi mystic Irina Tweedie spoke of two primal impulses we are born with: The first, to survive—to stay alive, to breathe. And the second, to praise—to praise and to pray to the Divine in all Their forms. Not in the forms that have been prescribed to us, but in all Their forms.

We come into this world carrying these two primal instincts. And just as this ancient memory buried within us must be nourished, so too must this ancient knowing that we come into this world with: the knowing of what it means to praise. As children we understand this innately. We know how to praise. We don't need words. We do not need to bow our heads and press our hands together. We do not need to learn a dogma or a system. This knowing is present within us. It is intimate and alive.

How many stories have we heard of children who say they talk to God? But they talk to God in all the ways that *they* feel called to, not in the ways that we are told we are supposed to talk to God. The ability to praise, to offer, to recognize what it means to be a human being is woven into us. Because we are part of this living, divine fabric of life, we must acknowledge it. We must give gratitude. We must be in relationship with it. And not from the mind or the layers of individual, cultural, or religious conditioning, but from the depth of who we really are: as a spirit, as a soul, so that spirit can meet spirit, the divine being that is our Earth. Because She is spirit, She demands to be met from our spirit. A prayer is essentially finding a way to access the spirit within and offering it to a greater spirit. Regardless of the tradition, prayer is a way of offering gratitude, of being in a space of reverence, and of creating a relationship. But prayer is not only an act of gratitude and reverence and asking for forgiveness—though it is all of these—it is also about making a relationship, validating a relationship, building a relationship, and making what has been severed whole again.

There are so many ways to praise. Over millennia, we have developed the most intricate, beautiful, and diverse expressions of praise. Some are secret, belonging to a people and a place and a culture, and should be kept as such. But some are universal: listening to the Divine, offering our thanks, asking for forgiveness. The last is important, because we have done so much that demands remorsefulness. These are universal ways of praise, universal ways of building a relationship. And if we integrate prayer and praise into our lives, whether we come from a faith-based tradition or not, we create space for the Earth's sacred presence within us to awaken, to become an embodied way of being. One does not simply pray once and say, *I've done that*. One returns again and again and again to offer praise, to offer thanks.

Yes, there are high days of worship. There are ceremonies. There are times of the year when special offerings can be made. But prayer should not be occasional; it should be constant and become a part of the way we live. It does not require words to be uttered. It can be as simple as recognition—seeing how She greets us as we move about our day in all the myriad ways She is present. Even in an urban setting, Her presence is all around us. We can hear birdsong in the busy streets. There are more ways to see Her than there are eyes with which to perceive Her. We walk upon Her with every step. We drink Her. We are nourished by Her as we eat our daily bread. And these are only a few examples. We cannot limit the ways we praise Her.

They say there are as many ways to praise God and reach God as there are human beings. But we have narrowed that understanding. We have confined the Divine to a transcendent God in heaven and abandoned the sacred beneath our feet. This ancient memory calls us back to the recognition that the Divine is also there beneath our feet. We can no longer ignore this. For our limited idea of the Divine is inseparable from the crises we now face. It is the responsibility of all—whether we are part of a faith tradition or not—to take this spiritual understanding seriously. We must evolve. We must return to this ancient knowing and integrate it into the reality of our lives as a response to this great crisis of our time. Because keeping the oil in the ground alone will not fix this crisis, nor will shifting to green and clean energy, or abandoning capitalism and facing the error of our ways, or reckoning with history and acknowledging what we have done to the planet and the people that make it their home. And while these things are all practical responses to the crisis we face and should be done, by themselves they are not enough. We must once again recognize the divine nature of this Earth and restore it to the foundation of who we are as human beings, as individuals, and, one day, as societies.

Prayer must be part of that. Prayer must not be made taboo, as it so often has been in an increasingly secularized modern world, partially because we have limited our understanding of prayer and of praise to something that must happen in a church on a Sunday or in a mosque five times a day. No. This ancient memory we hold within us, this innate understanding of praise, challenges that. In some ways we have to unlearn the systems of praise we have inherited in order to reclaim the true potential of a human being in praise. And the most amazing thing about prayer and praise is that they are never just about us. They do not exist solely to heal our own separation from the Earth, from this divine being that is our home. It *is* that, but it is much more.

This is where spirit and matter converge, not just in the healing of individuals but in the restoration of the whole. For if we are to survive and really heal, we must shift as a whole, which means our actions must benefit the whole. And prayer has the capacity to do this. Any real spiritual act, if it is offered from the depths of our being, from the heart, from something that is true within us, has the power to extend beyond ourselves. This is a spiritual technology. When we offer from a place of sincerity for the sake of others, for human beings and for more-than-human kin or even this great divine being that is the Earth Herself, its effects ripple outward: It benefits the whole.

We often hear about the insignificance of our individual choices when it comes to the environment. No matter how well we eat, how diligently we recycle, how often we take public transport or limit our air travel, those contributions will not make a real difference because the real change must come from system change, from policy change, from corporate change. And while that may be true in part, prayer offers something that *can* change the system—regardless of how small our contribution may seem. To me, prayer and praise are radical acts. If we don't limit them, they can be revolutionary. Each individual offering can benefit the whole and help heal the divide between spirit and matter. We can harness the spirit within us whether it arises through witnessing the beauty of Her bounty or from the depths of grief and pain over what we have done to Her. The spirit, when nourished and embodied through prayer, seeps into matter, like a strengthening bonding agent helping to mend the fracture. Each prayer can be an offering toward that healing.

The wounds are deep and the wounds are many. Prayer alone won't heal them. It must be done in concert, in combination, and in relationship with all the other things that we know must be done. But if prayer and praise and the recognition of creation's sacred nature lie at the root of our way of being, then all of our actions will emerge from that understanding. Then the values we need are obvious: reverence, interconnectedness, compassion, generosity, service. How could they be anything but? The action one takes will be naturally imbued with spirit, with love, as we offer it for the sake of the whole.

Sufis call themselves sweepers, for they devote their lives, through the power of remembrance, to sweeping away the dust of forgetfulness that has settled upon their hearts and upon the face of the Earth. Prayer is like that. Prayer is a sweeping away of forgetfulness because it is an honoring of remembrance. It is an affirmation, and affirmation is more powerful than negation. Threads of love woven through every prayer, through the ways we hold Her in our hearts, begin to mend the split between spirit and matter. They awaken this ancient memory of what spiritual ecology really is: spirit and home.

FOUR

An Offering of Remembrance

Beneath the ecological, cultural, and spiritual unraveling of our world, the Earth is crying out to be heard. She is calling us to step beyond the narrative that has brought us to the edge of the precipice where we now stand, the tale built on the illusion of control that is driving the mythic changes now gripping the planet: the warming climate, the fracturing ecosystems, the extinction of species. These great changes need our attention and response, but there is a deeper change that also needs to unfold. The deeper one is both a change of story and an inner shift, where we are no longer at the center—because we never belonged at the center of the story. But if we relinquish our place at the center, where do we turn? To whom do we turn? For me, the answer is clear: We turn toward the great, divine being that is our Earth. For the Earth is our Mother, our kin, and, in truth, ourselves.

When we remember this fundamental belonging, we begin the necessary inner shift of turning our gaze away from ourselves and toward Her, for She, who has always been the true center of our existence, is the space that holds us. When we make this shift, we enter a different space entirely. We step out of the familiar humancentric story and into a liminal space where human dominance fades—its days drawing to an end, even if its shadow still looms large—and something new quietly beckons us forward.

This is the journey unfolding: one world ending, another beginning. The shifts engulfing our outer world are inextricably linked to inner landscapes, those changing currents within our hearts and beings. They are two sides of the same transformation, unfolding together.

This new world is nascent, emerging like a tender shoot from the ashes of the old. It is not always visible, not always easy to discern, yet it calls to us. And to step into this emerging world we must let go of the old story. We must relinquish the role of protagonist and turn toward the great living Earth, the being whom we have perceived as the backdrop to our narrative but who is the story itself.

The Diné poet Natalie Diaz writes in her poem "The First Water Is the Body": *We must go beyond beyond to a place where we have never been the center, where there is no center—beyond, toward what does not need us yet makes us.*[4] The Earth does not need us in order to continue. She will go on, as She has for millennia, whether we remain or vanish. But there is a difference between being needed and being wanted. Her wanting is not possessive or dependent. Rather, it arises from the nature of relationship itself, because relationship is how life expresses its wholeness. When we step beyond ourselves as the center, we feel this. She wants us to engage, to relate, to remember that She is a great divine being who sustains us, who makes us. This is a perspective held within many Earth-based and mystical traditions. In Sufism, this is expressed through the famous *hadith qudsi* (meaning "a saying attributed to God through the Prophet Muhammad, peace be upon him"), which is central to Ibn 'Arabi's ontology of the Oneness of Being, expressing how God reveals itself to itself through creation: *I was a Hidden Treasure and I loved to be known, so I created the world that I might be known.*[5] The Earth's desire is an invitation, a call to participate, shown through Her generosity, kinship, and reciprocity, and through remembrance of the unity within all things. As Thomas Berry said when responding to the question, *What does the Earth desire?*

> I will put it in just a few short sentences . . . To be admired in her loveliness, to be tasted in her delicious fruits, to be listened to in her teaching, to be endured in the severity of her discipline, to be cared for as a

maternal source from whence we come, a destiny to which we return. It's very simple.[6]

How then do we orient ourselves in relationship to this great being that is our Earth, that is our Mother? Turning away from the collapsing world is not enough; it is merely the first step. The deeper question is how do we root ourselves in this emerging world that She is inviting us to step toward? How do we hold ourselves in relationship to Her? How do we praise Her?

For this we can look to the Earth Herself as a mirror, for She shows us an example of how to be. Every moment of every day, She gives of Herself unceasingly. Without Her we cannot breathe. Without Her we cannot eat. Without Her nothing is possible. Her offering is abundant, constant, and unconditional, a flowing gift that sustains all life. It does not abide by our rules, nor does it demand recognition. To orient ourselves to Her, we must ground our being in offering, as She does. Any true offering, if it is born from the depths of our being with sincerity, is not for us. It is for the *Earth*.

This is the orientation we must take: to offer ourselves as She offers Herself, without expectation or demand. To *root* ourselves in the act of giving, not for personal gain but in service to the Whole. In doing so, we hope to resist the pull of forgetfulness, the draw to humancentric ways of being that linger at the edges, tempting us to return to old patterns. Instead, we take the first step toward Her. We align ourselves with Her rhythms. We offer ourselves to Her, as She has always offered Herself to us.

"What can we offer Her?" we might ask, as She has all She needs. For me, we start by offering Her our humility and asking for forgiveness. *Forgive me, great Mother. Forgive me for what I have done, for how forgetful I have been. Forgive me, forgive me. Forgive me for what I have done, for my complicity in what has been done to you, for what I have allowed to unfold, for what I have watched being done to you.* And I don't just ask once or twice, I ask daily, because each day we can so easily forget and slip back into the old story.

From this space of forgiveness and humility we can offer our recognition of Her. And here it becomes a beautiful and unpredictable journey, because the ways that She offers Herself to us are so myriad they cannot be counted. There are too many ways to even comprehend, because She is present in everything: in every rising of the sun and setting of the moon, in every passing cloud and every tree and every blade of grass. And She wants us to recognize who She is in the smallest of ways, greeting and acknowledging Her through our senses, and in the most profound and miraculous ways, engulfed in a beauty that can never be described. We soak it all in, the mundane and the miraculous, and we recognize it as an expression, as an outpouring of Her. If we allow it, our recognition of this great being that is our

Mother can become the central defining way we live our lives. Not with ourselves at the center, but with the recognition that She is at the center in all the forms She takes.

When we wake up, we are given the opportunity to remember Her, to recognize Her. And as we go about our days, there are so many opportunities to engage the external senses in conscious awareness of Her ceaseless offerings. How we recognize the presence of a tree providing us shade on the street as we walk to work. How we hear the wind rustling through its branches, smell its blossoms in springtime and the decaying leaves at its base in autumn. How our skin feels warmth, rain, or a cool breeze. Everywhere you turn, there She is. Her abundance is overwhelming. And there is no excuse to ignore Her. Once one turns away from being at the center and looks toward Her and says, *I offer myself to you, just as you offer yourself to me*, there is no excuse to not recognize Her in all the ways She makes Herself known. Each time we forget to recognize, we are drawn back to being at the center of the story.

The more we recognize Her, the more our ability to be in a space of attentiveness to Her expands. It is as if the senses, which used to function only in their physical form—in our ability to see, hear, smell, taste, and touch—change to make way for the inner senses. The inner senses are not rooted in the physical body, but in the spirit. These senses are what the Sufis call the *eye of the heart* and the *ear of the heart*, which, if awakened, can bridge the worlds of spirit and matter and deepen our capacity to feel Her body, to feel Her spirit. This changes our ability to be in a space of attentiveness. And it changes our ability to notice what is happening beyond the headlines, as it allows us to actually witness and perceive with the full capacity that we have as human beings—with our physical eyes and our metaphysical eyes, our physical ears and the ears within. And then what we see and, more important, what we feel shift and change.

The news of ecological destruction and species extinction is then no longer just news. It reverberates through our very being not as distant headlines but as tremors ripping through us as they rip through Her. These tremors shake us to our core, as they should. When we allow ourselves to feel even a fraction of what She feels, it breaks us open. It leaves a mark, as it must.

From this breaking open, grief flows. Pain, desolation, disbelief—all these feelings arise, as they should. She feels them, and if we are to step out of the old story, we must feel them too so that we do not dare get caught once again in the grip of forgetfulness. We must be broken open by Her pain, by the cry of the Earth. For only then, when we are able to truly bear witness with our inner and outer senses, with the full capacity of our being, will we be able to step away from the old story and begin to again root ourselves in Her. Bearing witness in this way is not simply observing, not merely mourning from a distance. It is allowing the grief and pain to wash over us and through us so that we hold what has happened deep within ourselves. This is what it means to ask for forgiveness. It is to feel what She feels so that we may know. So that we may remember. So that we do not forget again.

It will hurt deeply. But if we truly offer ourselves, we can bear it. The human heart, when offered genuinely and sincerely, is much larger than we realize. The human body, when placed in the space of offering, has a greater capacity than we imagine. And when it is linked to the heart, together they can hold so much. And in holding this pain, this suffering, and this grief, something ancient is awakened within us—if we allow it.

When we allow ourselves to feel Her pain, Her cry, we feel vulnerable, just like She is vulnerable, and in that moment something profound happens. That vulnerability is like a key turning in a lock, opening a deep, ancient love that exists between us and Her, our Mother, this great divine being we call Earth. It is a love we may have felt before as we bathed in Her beauty, Her generosity, Her abundance. But when we feel Her pain, the quality of that love shifts. It becomes deeper, more potent. It has the capacity to become primordial, reconnecting us to a love that existed at the beginning, a love we forgot and buried beneath images of ourselves.

This love is the most wondrous thing. It is authentic and pure, and it taps into the most essential, primal aspect of who we are. It connects us to Her through the unseen relationship; it is the spirit that flows within the physical world amid the atoms we share and the air that surrounds us. And when this love awakens it transforms us. Our inner landscapes shift. The blood that runs through our veins becomes indistinguishable from the rivers that course through Her. This awakened love flows like water, binding us to Her in a relationship as old as time.

When love is present, everything changes. Our relationship to Her deepens. It shifts from something superficial that existed only on the surface to something profound and enduring. This love is unlike anything we have known; it is deeper than human romantic love, rendering it almost trivial by comparison. It is felt in our bones and the depths of our hearts. And when this love awakens, it does not easily fade. It transforms us, infusing every action with sacredness. The division between the sacred and the profane dissolves, for how could any act be anything but sacred when imbued with such love? Even the simple act of walking becomes an act of remembrance, a flowing connection to Her. In this state, prayers change, silence deepens, and even what some might perceive as inaction becomes charged with meaning. This love reshapes the very quality of our being, anchoring us in a deeper, truer relationship with Her.

From this relationship a space begins to open within us. This space is not fleeting or ephemeral; it is lasting and it is an offering. It is born from love, grief, recognition, and forgiveness and woven together into a container—a vessel that exists within our hearts. This vessel holds the sacred nature of creation within it. It is a space of remembrance, a temple where She is honored in both the smallest and largest ways.

This vessel grows with our love. It becomes an inner space of not only remembrance but of praise and of refuge, one that offers us sanctuary in a world consumed by forgetfulness. If we are to keep alive the sacred nature of creation and the thread of remembrance, we must actively, sincerely cultivate these spaces within us. Without them that sacred connection may slip away.

Yet this refuge is not merely for the present, not merely to help us navigate our way through the grief, loss, and love that we hold deep within. It must also hold something for the future. Like cathedral stones laid one generation after another, these spaces are built for a world that will emerge slowly, perhaps beyond our lifetimes. They must endure, holding the sacred through the transition, offering a seed of remembrance to the future.

Held within our hearts, these spaces are not solitary. Instinctively, they recognize the presence of other awakened hearts, other vessels. This is not merely intellectual; it is spiritual. Individual spirit threads of remembrance are woven together, functioning like a mycorrhizal network under a forest floor, connecting spaces of love offered toward Her, bound in service to the Whole. These awakened hearts can come together as both hidden and visible communities, the hidden reflecting an esoteric knowledge of that which cannot be seen, offering an important recognition of the sacred that benefits the Whole. The visible community emerges from this hidden network like mushrooms clustered together aboveground, offering an outer refuge and a physically embodied space of remembrance and love.

There is a line by Bertolt Brecht about how there will be singing in the dark times.[7] In the present, these spaces keep alive the note of remembrance and ensure that, even in this age of darkness, there will be songs. And they also serve as a foundation for the future, holding something sacred through the long transition ahead. To nurture these inner spaces, we must have the simple recognition of who She is in our practice. Without this offering of remembrance the potency of these spaces fades. They are sustained by turning toward Her, again and again. In the end this is not about us. We are the stewards of remembrance, the holders of these sacred threads. These spaces within us are offerings of love, offerings toward Her, woven into the great tapestry of creation.

The Axis of All Things

The great Sufi poet Jalāl al-Dīn Rūmī wrote, *Step out of the circle of time and into the circle of love.*[8] At their most essential, Rūmī's words are an invitation, a portal into a different way of seeing and being in relationship with the world that is far more expansive than the one we most often inhabit. It is a call to leave behind a human-centered frame of time, bound and linear, and to step into a frame that holds no bounds, for this is the circle of love.

All forms of time—be they markers of movement or change in the past, present, or future, earthbound or beyond—are cycles: From the smallest to the most grand, they exist in relationship with one another. From the mountain to the river, to the tree, to the cherry blossom at the height of its bloom, each is a cycle. Whether it lasts a minute, a day, or a thousand years, it is still a cycle. These cycles do not spin within a single dimension; they move through many dimensions, interwoven and dynamic. Time, in its true form, is not a marker of progress, it is a way of being. This is an important distinction. We have taken these cycles, these natural rhythms of existence, and forced them into linearity. What once functioned as interconnected and overlapping circles has been transformed into a straight line, a tool for measuring and marking progress. But this is an illusion. Time is not a straight line; it is a continuous, multidimensional experience of life.

Time's cycles are not only rhythms; they are expressions. They are attributes of the Earth Herself, representations of Her infinite creativity and vitality, manifest in more forms than we can count or even comprehend. If we look closely, we can see these cycles spinning all around us. They unfold in every moment, waiting to be noticed and marveled at. The diversity of time's expressions is infinite, transcending imagination—mountains and rivers, trees and flowers in full bloom, or birds whose songs fill the air during the dawn chorus. Each moment is its own cycle of time. And in these moments, the timeless and the timebound merge to form an experience of being. Each of Her expressions becomes a song—sometimes a chorus, vast and harmonious, sometimes a single note, clear and poignant.

But we have silenced these songs, as we have dismantled these cycles and forced them into straight lines, mechanized expressions of the fractured world we live in. The way we relate to time has become a reflection of our fragmented relationship with the living Earth and is a symptom of how we have moved from recognizing ourselves as part of a whole to placing ourselves on the throne atop the pyramid of life. Once, we observed and acknowledged these cycles, lived in relationship with them, and attuned ourselves to their rhythms. Now, we barely see them, even when they are right before us. Instead we see only our own reflection. We have turned time into a system of control, a system to subjugate, colonize, and capitalize, as we have done to so many of Earth's cycles. In doing so, we've desacralized what is sacred. These cycles, limitless and boundless expressions of the Earth, have been flattened. Stripped of their vitality, their multiplicity, their deep connection to place, they have been reduced to a single uniform expression: a relentless ticking clock. Even the cycle of day and night, once intimately guiding our lives, has been severed, no longer aligning us with the light and darkness of the Earth's circadian rhythms. This kind of time, removed from the Earth it once reflected, is now as unyielding as the lights of our twenty-four-hour modern clocks. It has become a symbol of separation, and it holds us prisoner.

But of course this story of time is only one chapter in a larger story of forgetfulness. The loss of what time truly is reflects something that has enveloped our entire world. At its heart, it is a story of desacralization. It is the forgetting of the sacred nature of creation, of the true essence of the

Earth and the myriad ways She expresses Herself through time. Yes, it is also a story of violence, of domination, of oppression, of the turning of everything and everyone into something to be controlled, exploited for profit and greed. It is all of those things. But what lies at the root? Every cycle, every rhythm, every expression of Her has been desacralized. And among these expressions, time is one of the most foundational.

Time is not simply a tool for control. Time is a multidimensional expression of mystery, an infinite unfolding that exists in more forms than we can ever comprehend. And yet we have stripped this mystery bare, torn it from its roots, simplified it, and claimed ownership over it. What was once a sacred expression has been reduced to something utilitarian, something bound and isolated. But nothing exists in isolation. This is a fundamental truth of existence, whether understood ecologically or spiritually. Time encompasses both the physical and the metaphysical. It is both simultaneously: a great conversation of cycles meeting cycles, of inner meeting outer.

We ourselves are layers of cycles, from the most primal cycle of the in- and out-breath that is expressed seventeen thousand times a day to the circadian rhythms within the twenty-four hours the Earth spins on its axis to the hormonal cycles that regulate our biology, perhaps most obvious with a woman's menstrual cycle. Encompassing all of those is the cycle of our lifespan, echoing the seasonal journey of birth, growth, decay, and death that unfolds all around us as we circumambulate the sun. We are many cycles, just as the cherry blossom at the height of its bloom is part of countless cycles and the mountain, layered with rock upon rock over thousands of years, is a cycle within cycles. The tree relates to the mountain, the cherry blossoms to the river as it flows from its source to the sea. These cycles are not limited by the boundaries we impose. They exist outside of space, beyond our concepts, in a vast, interconnected field of relationship that includes us.

But this field of relationship has been silenced. In the same way the voices of the living world that have filled the air since time immemorial are now being silenced, so too are these cycles. To me, this is a central aspect of the desacralization of the living Earth and all that is a part of Her.

To understand what this means, we first need to see clearly what lies beneath the surface of what is unfolding, because what we are facing is not simply an ecological crisis or an economic crisis or a social crisis or a political crisis. It is all of these things. But at its root, it is a spiritual crisis. It is also a response, pointing the way toward repairing what has been severed, showing us how removed we've become from what is most primal: our connection with the Earth, our kinship with Her. We have allowed ourselves to fall into illusions of grandeur, to believe that we could flatten time, turn cycles into a straight line, and impose ourselves on the sacred. What hubris. What arrogance!

For too long we have been taught to say: *We are not the Earth. We are above that.* And in that severance—spirit torn from matter—we convinced ourselves that we could do anything. But when we open ourselves to this realization, we are led down a deeper road to ask: *What is at the core of both spirit and matter? What is at the core of the sacred nature of creation? What is at the core of every cycle of time?*

Rūmī left us a hint: *Step out of the circle of time and into the circle of love.* Because at the core of everything—the sacred nature of creation, every cycle of time—there is love. Not love in the limited sense of our human-centered experience, but love as the axis of all things. This is love as an energy, a force that flows between the physical and the metaphysical. It is the essence that binds spirit and matter together, holding them in unity like an invisible glue. This love is not confined; it permeates everything. It exists inside of us in countless ways, just as it exists inside every form of creation. It is present in every cycle of time. In the cherry blossom, at the height of its bloom, at its withering into seed, there is love. This love is the foundation, the axis, the essence. It is what connects all things, sustains all things, and reminds us of the sacred nature of existence.

This is the even deeper crisis that has unfolded: forgetting that love is the central axis of all things and forgetting that love is present in everything. We have not only tried to control time, we have even tried to control love. We have made love a human experience limited to our romantic or familial relationships. And while those expressions of love are beautiful and valuable, they are limiting if we think love is only this.

This journey of remembrance, then, which encompasses far more than just Earth Time, is about rediscovering this core truth, this axis that lies at the heart of all existence. It is about reawakening something that has always been inside of us, even if it lies dormant, hibernating, waiting for us to realize it is there. This is the primal covenant of relationship that has always existed, binding every single thing on this Earth together—a covenant we have buried under layers of forgetfulness, greed, and the arrogance that led us to believe we could control the most fundamental ways of being, that we could alter the fabric of creation, flatten time, and claim dominion over what is far beyond our comprehension. And in our endless quest to discover everything, we have forgotten the importance of mystery. We have discarded the value of the unknown. In doing so, we have lost sight of what cannot and should not be known but that must be respected.

This unraveling we are living through now is also a process of humility. It is calling us to remember how little we truly know, to recognize that we do not even understand how to care for what cares for us. And yet we continue to press forward recklessly, casting mystery aside, ignoring the living Earth, and carving a straight line of so-called progress that cuts deeper and deeper as it unfolds.

It's time to take the blinders off, time to stop limiting our own understanding of what this world is. When we awaken to a truth so essential and engage with it fully, the transformation can be immediate, and then magic can come alive. This is very important. I don't mean magic in any sort of limited, trivial, hocus-pocus way. I mean magic as love—the force that binds spirit and matter together, the dance that exists between all forms of creation.

This dance plays out effortlessly all around us, yet we must make an effort now to engage, to remember what magic truly means. Love is the fabric, the thread, and the needle that can weave spirit and matter together, that can help unfurl time like a spiral and return it to its natural cycle. Once this love is present, the ancient covenant of relationship reveals itself. We don't have to create it or build it. It is already there. The veil is lifted through the remembrance of love. This is a fundamental mystical truth—one that has been expounded in every form of mysticism and spiritual life across time and cultures. All roads lead back to this core truth. It is as present in the ecological world around us as it is in the human heart. This essence of love, when we turn toward it, ignites the magic that weaves a spell to bind the worlds back together.

As part of this, there is healing that must unfold within our most foundational ways of being, of which time is one. We must look at these primal and foundational ways, uncover what we have hidden, and remember, again and again, what is at their essence. We must weave this thread of love back into the core of the world through the simple awakening of what is most essential inside of us: the fundamental truth that love exists. Love is there. You don't even have to look deeply to find it. Love as an energy. Love as a source. Love as the central building block, the ingredient present in everything. The interconnectedness we see all around us, whether in the mycelial networks beneath the forest floor or the way water becomes vapor, cloud, and rain over and over again, is a reflection of something deeper, more foundational, more primal. It is the braiding together of spirit and matter that love makes possible. Because it is love that functions as the mycelial network; it is love in the cycle of water, in the rising and setting of the sun, in the phases of the moon, in the generations of cherry trees and each of their blossoms.

All of these cycles mirror the ways that love expresses itself inwardly. Yet we have forgotten these truths as well. We have forgotten those forms of time. Everything has become so dry, so predictable, so devoid of life, so stripped of mystery. But the magic of love, the magic of time, is still there. If we begin to see it for what it is, to actively participate in its remembrance, we can bring it alive once more. And here lies an important distinction: We must move from being observers to being participants.

We cannot stand on the sidelines merely looking in. Even if we come to recognize that these forms are cycles, that these cycles are expressions of time, and that these expressions of time are ultimately expressions of Her love, it is not enough to just see them. We must *engage* with them. We cannot simply seek connection with nature. We must participate in communion with nature. Spiritual ecology is about communion as much as it is about love, as much as it is about braiding together the worlds of spirit and matter and returning to an understanding of the sacred nature of creation.

Communion is essential because love does not exist in isolation. Love exists in relationship, just as time exists in relationship, just as the cherry blossom exists in relationship. And real relationships are ultimately about communion. Communion does not belong solely in a church, mosque, or temple. It does not reside only on a meditation cushion, in the prayers we utter, or even within our hearts. It is alive, as alive as the Earth, as alive as creation itself. But for it to unfold as it is meant to, we must stop limiting, controlling, or turning away from it. We often speak of the animate nature of creation, of the living Earth and the voices of the more-than-human world. We stress the importance of recognizing their aliveness. But if we do not ask what lies beneath that aliveness, we remain on the sidelines. To be participants we need to go deeper and ask: *What does it mean to be alive?*

Too often we answer this question from a single perspective: from a material perspective, not a spiritual one. But this question demands to be answered from a spiritual perspective. Spirit and matter must be braided back together. This is the work: to braid those worlds together, to remember the sacred nature of creation, and in doing so, to restore the rhythms belonging to Earth Time to their rightful place in the great web of being.

To recognize and participate in even one cycle can break the dam and allow what flows naturally to flow once again. It doesn't take much: One does not need to embark on a lifelong mystical journey. Rather, it begins with a simple act of remembrance and the willingness to follow that remembrance. The cycles already exist within us, waiting for our attention. *We* are cycles of time; whether it's the rhythm of our heartbeat, the daily cycle of waking and sleeping, or the lifelong arc of birth to death, these are ancient cycles deeply aligned with the Earth. If we place our attention there, on the breath, on the heartbeat, and allow them to guide us, to do their work and let the mind be quieted, something extraordinary happens. These inner cycles naturally begin to align with and respond to the cycles around us. That is the beauty of it and also the science—the mystical science.

This is not a new discovery. These are the same cycles that have guided cultures, traditions, and spiritual systems around the world for millennia in braiding together the worlds. These cycles help us lift the veil and step out of our limited sense of self to experience a world much more porous and expansive than we can imagine. But if we remain caught in forgetfulness rather than embracing remembrance and the cycles that are already inside of us, we may never find our way there.

The heartbeat and the breath—breathing in, breathing out—help us to recognize what it truly means to hold the worlds together; they help us to realize how ancient and how primal these rhythms are. Behind every breath is the same substance of creation. It has many names. Some call it *prana*, some call it *chi*. I call it love. Love exists in every cycle of time and every form of creation. It is the axis of all things. Step out of the circle of time and step into the circle of love. When you step away from your ego self, a world of mystery and magic unfolds. A world of creation and destruction, of cycles upon cycles beginning and ending, interweaving and unfolding in relationship. This hidden world where spirit is woven between everything doesn't need to remain hidden. The breath, the heartbeat, the movement of one footstep in front of another—these simple cycles are fundamental ways that human beings live and mark time. But they are also expressions of mystery. They hold the potential to be keys that unlock our capacity to step into deeper cycles, to remember Earth Time.

Through these cycles we can participate in a process of healing and reconnection. We not only understand the crisis and respond outwardly, but we can become part of the healing itself. By simply attending to the in-breath and the out-breath, or the beat of the heart, by returning to these ancient rhythms and activating them within ourselves, we awaken what has always been present. For it is through the mystery of time that we remember we are of the Earth, part of the endless turning of the wheel, the continuous rhythm, the call and the echo.

Learning to Be a Lover

For me, the Earth is an aspect of my Beloved, the great unknowable mystery and creator known by many names. She is a life-giving creative force and divine being—the great seductress. Given enough time, She will draw anyone into Her embrace. It does not matter where we come from or how distant from the land our life has been. Once the Earth begins Her process of seduction, the pull is inevitable, irresistible. She enraptures us with Her presence, Her beauty, Her depth.

The Earth's love surrounds us constantly, as a presence looking upon us with countless eyes and a love that longs to meet our gaze, to pull us from the confines of our personal, familial, and cultural conditioning. To step into this gaze is to move into vulnerability, to enter the space of mystery and the unknown, away from the security of all we have been taught to cling to. This is the beginning of how we learn to be a lover: to open our eyes, open our ears, and allow our very pores to feel the presence of that love seeping in with every breath we take, moving in and out like the rhythm of life itself.

But once Her gaze fixes upon us and we dare to meet it, a different journey begins. A different dance unfolds. A relationship is born—or at least its beginnings. For the Sufi, this relationship is always with the Beloved and all the forms they take, earthly and beyond. They say in all the universe there are only two, lover and Beloved. And the only way to be with the Beloved is to be a lover.

In times of crisis we are called to remember what it means to be a lover, to remember how to love this great, indescribable Earth who encompasses all of us. To be a lover is no small thing. It requires commitment, presence, and devotion. It asks us to shed selfishness, laziness, and inconsistency. We cannot be lovers only on Wednesdays or only when it is convenient. We are asked to be lovers every day, in every moment, responding to Her ever-changing whims. Finding that space of connection is not always easy, especially in this era of forgetfulness. Ours is a world of mirrors—cities of mirrors, societies of mirrors—all reflecting back our own image, the human gaze, endlessly turned toward itself.

To be a lover in this world, we must turn away from these mirrors. We must shift our gaze outward, beyond ourselves, toward Her. We must learn to see again, to feel again, to love again. And in doing so, we may find our way back to the great seductress who has always been waiting, Her love infinite, Her gaze unwavering.

If we stand in a field or forest with our ears and hearts open and we listen to birdsong, something happens. It stirs us. It opens our hearts and makes us want to respond, to become lovers too. Just as we feel the breath of a human lover on our neck—the intimacy, the yearning, the longing, the passion, the love—all these feelings are present when the wind moves through the branches of a tree or brushes over the meadow beneath it, soft and tender.

It's all there in the wind that is also the breath, in the birdsong and starlight. These moments that enchant us can feel rare and precious. And yet they are all around us if we allow ourselves to hear and see them. But to recognize this, to truly feel it, takes time. It takes attention and dedication to remind ourselves how to love when the lover does not take the form of a human being. We are so accustomed to a narrow understanding of love, so conditioned by a limited view of intimacy, that we often fail to notice these gestures of love all around us. We are so predisposed by our preferences for the living world to express itself in ways that are comfortable to us that we forget that She is equally present on a frigid winter morning, in a bitter wind, or in the heat and humidity of a scorching summer day.

We are being asked to expand our understanding of love, to broaden our notion of intimacy, and to step into the space of learning how to be a lover again, not just with another human being but with the vast, infinite, and intimate presence of the Earth Herself. What are the qualities we need to cultivate to become lovers? Simple practices are gateways. Whether we walk through a landscape, follow a path, or move in celebration, these practices open the door. That celebration does not always take the form of outward expression; often it is within the inner landscape of the heart that this celebration unfolds.

When we walk with remembrance of who we really are, aware of where we are and with whom, we begin to see the world differently. How would you walk across a lover's back? How would you breathe in the presence of a lover? One would hope with tenderness.

Tenderness is essential. Through the incredible harshness of the realities we face, the grief we feel, the Earth's cries that echo through us, there is also a softness awakening. It emerges quietly, yet it holds great power in its deep vulnerability and openness.

To be tender, to be truly open in the way She asks of us—the way a Beloved asks of their lover—is humbling. It requires a radical vulnerability, a willingness to place ourselves fully in that openness no matter how raw or exposed it may make us feel. To be tender one must *be* tender. There is no room for hiding in tenderness. Walls, veils of separation, masks of protection all must fall away. To be truly present, to truly offer ourselves to Her, we must reveal everything about ourselves. Anything less is a partial gaze, a conditioned response and meeting that lacks sincerity.

To be a lover is to show ourselves in all our imperfections and frailties, to meet Her gaze without walls, without false eyes or veils of protection. She asks us to come as we are, with the openness and frailty of our real nature, even if we are wounded. Especially if we are wounded. It is through Her own woundedness that She reveals the need for us to step into Her light, holding our own wounds with open hands and open hearts.

At this time there is so much we can learn about the importance of these fundamental ways of being, and yet they are not merely human ways of being. We are being taught how to be human so that we can learn how to fully recognize the more-than-human. This paradox is part of the mystery, part of the secret. Thich Nhat Hanh expresses this beautifully:

> You are present in every cell of my body. My physical body is your physical body, and just as the sun and stars are present in you, they are also present in me. You are not outside of me and I am not outside of you. You are more than just my environment. You are nothing less than myself.[9]

Where does the journey of lover and Beloved lead us? To separation? No. When lovers come together embracing tenderness, vulnerability, and openness, they become as one. There is union. Once you have experienced it, you long to experience it again and again. Why? Because it is real. And this dance that She leads us in is not a linear path, it is a spiral. It draws us closer and closer to Her, and in doing so it draws us closer and closer to ourselves. Once we step into this realization, this real acknowledgment that separation is an illusion and that union is the true nature of reality, everything changes. Then one brings a level of consciousness and awareness to the true nature of reality and Her presence here.

One needs patience and attentiveness for the journey. Compassion and generosity. All the values that are worth striving toward have to be embodied. We have to earn it. The journey is a long and winding one, but it is the only journey that truly matters. Because if She is present in every cell of our bodies, in every atom, every particle, and every blood vessel, then we embody the essence of relationship. We acknowledge the true nature of creation, not just intellectually but with every breath, every step.

As we step into this space, we reflect a quality of Her nature back into creation, back into the world. It's a different set of mirrors than those we've built around ourselves, a different way of working with light. Our remembrance of Her reflects remembrance into a space of forgetfulness. This is the power of a human being. When we are not only centered on being human, we become a space of reflection, a conduit of light, a vessel for a story, and so much more. And that is also the work—to recognize the importance and power and potency of that reflection in an era of forgetfulness. It is a privilege to have felt Her gaze and a responsibility to return it.

And while one can feel the great benefits of Her gaze and the embrace of that love and the beauty and the rapture and the terror and the awe and the majesty, and all the qualities that are exhibited as She twirls and twirls and twirls like a dancer, it is a great responsibility to not make it only about our own well-being but to always hold it within a larger container, a larger understanding that says it is not about us. Because if She is present in every cell of my body, if my physical body is Her physical body, then how can it be only about me?

All the practices and values we strive to embody are leading us toward the ultimate acknowledgment: the recognition of union. She is alive in the very center of our being, just as She is alive in the treetops that sway in the wind. The same life animates both, the same essence flows through all. And She will eventually ensnare us all. This is the relationship of lover and Beloved. And this is the truth we are called to remember.

SEVEN

Embracing Limitations

Once we have cultivated a relationship with the great seductress, the Earth, how do we keep it alive? With this question comes a subtle danger: the temptation to create constraints and limitations on how we live this relationship.

This relationship is not meant to be confined to moments of stillness. It is not bound to the quiet sanctuaries where Her presence feels strongest, where trees drown out the noise of cars, where there are no airplanes overhead, and where birdsong fills the dawn. These sacred spaces draw us into intimacy with Her. They envelop us. They are intoxicating. They remind us of how it once was, everywhere. In these moments it feels effortless to hear Her voice, to sense Her presence, to be nourished by Her, and to nourish Her in return. But there is a danger in romanticizing this experience, in believing that it is only in such spaces—quiet, green, and seemingly untouched—that we can truly be in relationship with Her. It is tempting to say: *Here, I can re-*

member. Here, I can be as I once was. Here, I am surrounded by spirit and the reflection of what I long to feel. In the city, with its relentless clamor reverberating all around us, and its ever-present glow of screens, it may seem harder to connect, harder to hear, harder to be in relationship. But there is hubris at the heart of this thinking.

Spaces of sanctuary that are less impacted by the modern world, both human and more-than-human, are vital. They remind us, support us, and sustain us. They hold great value. But to think that our relationship with Her is dependent on such spaces puts a constraint on something limitless. If She is everywhere, including within us, then placing limitations on how and where we perceive or engage with Her is an insult. It reduces Her vastness to the conditions of our comfort and convenience. And in doing so, it places the human back at the center. It says: *I can be in relationship with You when You are all around me, when You envelop me with Your beauty and stillness. But when it becomes harder, when the noise of the world grows louder, when the green hills fade into suburbia, I cannot.* This is arrogance. If She is everywhere, then our relationship with Her must find its way into the very bones of our everyday lives. Anything less diminishes the boundlessness of Her presence and the fullness of what it means to love Her.

There is a real power in learning to be attentive to Her gaze when we have to enter a space where She is not as abundant as She should be. These spaces challenge us. They force us to be attentive in the way we were when She first captured our attention. So we are attentive not only when Her presence is obvious but also when it is more subtle, more hidden.

But in truth, how hidden are the sky and the clouds? How hidden are the sun, the moon? Instead of recognizing the grandeur of what is offered in every waking moment of our lives, we focus on what is absent. We say: *This place is not green enough. There are not enough trees. The noise is too much.* We center ourselves in the narrative, bringing our own needs and preferences back to the forefront. And in doing so we forget. We forget that She is trying to teach us that there is no center, not in the way we understand it.

Do we want more trees? More green? More abundance? More biodiversity? Yes, yes, of course! But as we make this journey to unravel the web of forgetfulness we have become encased in, we can remember that every moment, every space, offers us an opportunity to be in relationship with Her—not only in the extraordinary but in the overlooked. It is easy to say: *A beautiful moonrise, a soft, lush, green hillside—these embrace me.* But what about the moment when you walk from your door to the subway station? In that journey, if you look closely, you pass as much wonder as you do on the hillside. And therein lies a lesson.

As we seek to recognize the living Earth everywhere, including in the concretized, brutalized landscapes of our modern world, we must also be confronted with what we have done. We must hold the paradox: the pain of our complicity alongside the beauty of Her continual offering. Perhaps in the cracks and corners of the everyday we are called to look more closely, more attentively, as if through a magnifying glass. To see what has always been there, waiting for our recognition.

A friend once described walking around their neighborhood block with their two young toddlers whose small steps turned the short circuit into an hour-long journey. Through the eyes of their children, they began to see the neighborhood differently. What once seemed like a constrained, concrete space, a built environment imposed upon the natural world, became something else entirely. The magic of a single flower, the quiet grace of a tree whose roots cracked the concrete paver stones, suddenly revealed themselves anew. What had appeared as a limitation transformed into an experience full of wonder.

Yes, we may long for a world where our built environments—our cities and homes—are designed with reverence for the living world. A world like the gardens of old Babylon, where human ingenuity worked in harmony with nature's abundance. That is the hope we carry. But even in the imperfect spaces we inhabit now, there is something to be learned in allowing Her myriad forms to be seen as they are, for wherever we are, She is there too.

If this is true, constraints then become vehicles of transformation. Without constraints we often grow lazy, complacent, even greedy. But when we are called to seek Her out in spaces where we must look harder, the act itself becomes an opportunity for change. In those moments we are taught to be grateful not only for Her presence but for Her seeming absence. It is in the spaces where She feels less tangible—amid the concrete, the chaos, the noise of our cities and our own minds—that we can begin to see Her anew.

When we feel Her less, it releases a kind of yearning, a deep longing that grows in Her absence. When our cups overflow with Her abundance, it is easy to feel connected. But in Her perceived absence, the longing that arises draws us closer. It sharpens our focus, makes us more attentive, and helps us break free from the patterns of humancentric thought. This cycle of abundance, scarcity, and longing shifts how we relate to Her. We begin to approach Her differently, not as something to be projected on, but as She is, on Her own terms.

This is how the constraints we face, whether physical, environmental, or psychological, can begin to unseat the human from the center. They spin us out of that false position, forcing us to stand humbly to the side, in awe of Her. No longer do we demand that She make us feel better or satisfy our desires. Instead we ask simply for Her presence, to witness Her in Her time, Her place, Her way.

But this is not easy. It requires daily attention to resist falling into patterns of forgetfulness or resentment. *Why do I live here? I wish I lived there; it would be easier to feel Her there.* These thoughts insist on a set of conditions for connection. True relationship does not depend on ideal circumstances. It does not demand the idyllic backdrop of an untouched forest or a meadow fragrant with wildflowers. Let such moments of beauty be what they are: gifts, opportunities to be nourished by Her bounty. Hold them as memories, but do not let them overshadow the everyday opportunities to experience Her presence. She is also present in the cracks of a sidewalk where the grass and weeds take root, in the concrete itself that is made of sand and water, and in the glint of sunlight on a skyscraper's glass window encased in steel that was mined from the depths of the Earth.

And even if you do not yet have the eyes to perceive Her subtle beauty, does that mean you cannot feel it? If you do not yet have the ears to hear Her whispers, does that mean you are deaf to it? No. You can sense it if you quiet your mind and open your heart. Even in the most unexpected places—a packed subway car, an office cubicle, high in a skyscraper—She is present. To say *I cannot be with Her here* is to make it about yourself, to place conditions on the relationship. And in doing so, the lesson She is teaching can only go so far.

The recognition that She is everywhere and nowhere, above and below, must become the center. Not a center that elevates the human, but a center that grounds us in the truth of Her presence. If this understanding becomes the foundation of our being, then everything in our lives begins to realign to that truth. It shifts perception. It transforms how we see, how we move, how we live. It changes everything, if we allow it.

As Thich Nhat Hanh reminds us, She is present in every cell of our being. But to turn our gaze inward must not become an act of self-centeredness. To truly see Her within ourselves is to see beyond ourselves. There are layers upon layers to the circle She is teaching us, which spins in constant variation and unfurls like a spiral that draws us closer to what lies beyond human understanding.

She *is* us. And while She does not need us in the way we understand need, we need Her. She calls us to acknowledge Her, to remember Her, to witness Her, to feel Her presence in our waking hours and in our dreams. To have Her as the first thought when we rise and the last before we sleep. And yet She exists far beyond the bounds of our need. Every time we attempt to define Her, we limit Her. She is so much greater than we can imagine.

Even in the barren wastelands of our destruction, She is present. In the ashes of the trees that have burned, in the bodies of the birds that have fallen, She remains. She is present in the concrete beneath our feet as much as in the green of the leaves or the hum of the bees. She is in the rocks and the sand, in all that we have made—even in what we have twisted and desecrated. We cannot escape Her, nor can we limit Her. This is part of the lesson She is teaching us: to recognize Her in everything, even where we least expect it.

Grief, witnessing, remembrance, love, and acknowledgment. Each is vital, but they must never be about us. To truly hold these acts in their fullness, we must hold Her first. Witness for Her sake. Grieve for Her sake. Love for Her sake. In doing so, She reveals within us the love that is Her own.

In striving to live this way, something remarkable happens. Our sight sharpens. Our hearing deepens. Our senses awaken. The veil of separation lifts, and what is revealed is beyond anything we could imagine: a new level of Her beauty, Her presence, Her power, Her rage. The unknown becomes known, not because we have conquered it but because we have surrendered to it.

And so we must live as though She is the center—not in the human sense of domination or control but in the deeper truth of belonging. We must step beyond ourselves to a place where we have never been the center and where we never need to be.

EIGHT

Time and Place

To engage with the essence of Earth Time is to recognize its deep relationship with place. To fully engage requires intimacy. This intimacy, in turn, opens us to the love flowing through everything, the love at the heart of the sacred nature of creation. Love is the cycle, the space within the cycle, and the movement of the cycle itself. Whatever shape the cycle takes—a moment, a season, an eon—love remains at its center. It is the axis of all things. Time, too, is one of love's forms, containing layers and expressions beyond what we can imagine. Yet its essence remains unchanged, as it does in all forms.

When we attune ourselves to *Earth Time*—the cyclical, living rhythms of the world—we begin to recognize that spirit and matter have never been separate. But recognition alone is not enough; we are called to participate in this relationship, to live in a way that honors both the visible and the unseen. This is the work of mending what has been unnaturally ruptured. It requires a deep attunement to the rhythms that have always held us, an openness to the magic they hold, and the core ingredient of this magic is love. This braiding is done through offering, prayer, and praise, and through a rekindling of the cycles that lie dormant within. As we turn toward the rhythms that shape the living world, we learn again how to relate, to embrace, and ultimately to commune with Her. In doing so, we expand our understanding of time beyond the limits imposed by our hubris—beyond the straight lines, the boxes, and all they carry—so that time may once again be experienced in its fullness.

If we wish to move beyond these limitations, we can begin with the cycles within us—returning to the rhythm of our breath, the beat of our heart, the cadence of our step. Each of these brings us closer. But these cycles are only the surface. Beneath them is the love that truly connects us to these rhythms. This is what we are being asked to return to—the essential nature of all things.

This return is not for us alone. It is not only for our own healing or awakening, but for something greater, for the mutual reciprocity that arises when love is met with love. Every rhythm is part of a larger rhythm. Every cycle is nested within another. The day, the year, the century, the moment—each exists in concert, each is interwoven. And when love spins into love, it sets something in motion: a chain reaction, a remembering.

If love is the ingredient we are trying to work with, even if it feels abstract at first, reaching for it is still worthwhile. Love is always worth reaching for. But if we are to work with love, if we are to reach beyond the boundary of self into the boundless reality of Her bounty, how do we do so? Love takes many forms, but intimacy must be at the foundation of our relationship with the world around us, the forms of time, and the beings within it.

If we are truly seeking kinship, if our senses are to awaken to it, if our cycles are to draw us toward it as our rhythm meets the rhythm of another, then there must be intimacy. To be kin is to know one's kin. And to truly know another is to be intimate. It requires vulnerability, offering, and space. There is no taking. A true act of intimacy, when freely given, is an offering, never a possession.

Intimacy is one of the most beautiful and foundational expressions of love. It draws one toward another. It pulls, and it is pulled. It is not a solitary experience but a dance, and even at times a seduction—not in the sense of conquest, but as a mutual invitation, an unfolding. You are seducing and you are being seduced. And in the space between, intimacy emerges. There is love, there is kinship, there is knowing. Through that knowing and kinship, something within us is revealed, awakened only in relationship to the other—to that form, that cycle, that expression of time.

Every cycle holds more cycles than we can see, layers we can't fathom. As we deepen our attention, a cycle expands beyond what we can perceive. A single circle becomes a thousand, then a million, with no end. Intimacy does not arrive at a stopping point. The axis of all things has no limit, whether in undiluted essence or manifest form.

This coming to know through intimacy leads to something lasting. There is a difference between nature connection and nature communion. You connect; you forget. You commune; you remain. You are changed by the experience, and you do not forget. A bond forms. Kinship is not an idea or a concept. You are bonded to kin. It is like blood. And through remembering these forms of time, these cycles, these ways of relating, these ancient bonds can be reawakened, reformed, remade through intimacy. Awareness, yes. Attention, yes. Consciousness, yes. But those only bring one closer to the threshold. To cross, one must leave oneself slightly outside the room and enter—not for one's own sake but for the sake of the relationship that is waiting.

And when that bond takes root in the heart, the body, and even the mind—it stays. It leaves a trace, a residue, a layer of connection. Something is imprinted. And when something is imprinted, it cannot so easily be erased. The substance of that form is imprinted in the substance of your form. The rhythm of its cycle becomes part of your cycle. Cycle meets cycle. Form meets form. And the essence of both is the same.

Because the essential nature of all things—the axis of all things—is love, it flows. Form and emptiness shift, yet the axis remains. Love takes on many shapes, but it is always present. And so the bond that is made is imprinted. There is a specificity to the way this imprint is left in your being. It is not abstract. Because the relationship between time and place is linked, what unfolds in a cycle, in a form, is shaped by place. And when you engage with a cycle in a particular place, the imprint it leaves is tied to that place as a thread that leads you back to its origin.

One can relate to an oak tree anywhere in the world that an oak tree stands. And a kinship can form when one moves beyond the self toward that oak, allowing the ancient language of love to reignite what was always there. But that kinship does not connect you to every oak tree in the same way, because each is different—each is in relationship with its specific place. There is specificity in the way this language of love imprints upon your being, forming a bond between you and the other, but also tying you to the land itself. That place becomes known to you through the imprint of those forms upon your form. That oak tree becomes part of you, and you become part of that oak tree.

This was the way time, place, and beings once existed in relationship. It was simple, unfolding without the domination of the mechanistic model that overwhelms our world today. Life moved differently then. This natural flow wound its way through daily life, rooting one in the landscape as it rooted one's ancestors. Their relationship with the land, carried through ancestral memory, became part of you. And as you walked that landscape, imprinting a relationship with each step you took, the cycles of time absorbed into your being, deepening your connection to place.

Time is place-specific. But now we say: *It is the same here as it is anywhere. It is atomic time. It is not place-based time.* And that is dangerous. When ties of kinship, threads of love, and imprints of relationship are severed from what grounds them, we become unmoored. We are now mostly a society drifting, untethered from place.

The journey of healing, transformation, return, and remembrance requires reigniting that ancient relationship with place, but not as it was before, because our world is not as it was before. We may not live in one landscape for a lifetime. Our families come from many places. Our ancestral memory carries imprints from a mosaic of lands. But even so, we must return to an understanding of the relationship between time and place.

We can form a bond with a landscape even in passing, as visitors who linger for a few days. We are not trespassers; we are participants, acknowledging time as it reveals itself within place. Not imposing our own concept of time upon the land, but recognizing that time itself is an expression that emerges uniquely in each moment. This is where mystery enters. Because to truly begin to sense how time and place weave together is to stand on the edge of something vast, something beyond us.

Time, place, kinship, and the cycles and rhythms of creation all flow in concert. And while we may grasp the enormity of this remarkable symphony of continuous exchange in part, we can never fully understand it. That is what makes it so magical, so mysterious. But we can still receive its imprint, allowing it to work upon us. And that imprint comes through intimacy—which is an expression of love. As bonds of kinship deepen through this imprint, ties to place deepen as well. Intimacy forms not only with a particular being—an oak tree, for instance—but with the landscape surrounding it. Because love flows through intimacy, it offers a gateway to the other cycles that exist in relationship to that specific form. And so the landscape becomes accessible through our attention and relationship to that form. The place becomes accessible, its doors open to you. If you let it, it can become part of you, even if at first it is only a shallow imprint, a faint impression that must be deepened, layered upon, built over time.

Even within the fractured world we inhabit, this relationship to time and place still holds power. We do not have to wait for an ideal version of the world to emerge before we begin to engage in this ancient knowing again. The way home, the road out of this madness, is in learning to bridge the broken worlds. We are broken too. Engaging with time itself in this way is a way to heal, a way to help us find light within the darkness of this moment. Even for those of us who have been severed from our ancestral relationship to place, this knowing remains. The memory of what it means to be in relationship to land can be awoken again so that time is no longer abstract but rooted.

Remembering Earth Time is also about remembering Her—this great being that is the Earth. Earth Time is the way She spins within the cycles. We remember Her *in time*. We remember Her *through place*, through the forms of a place and their cycles. And with each return we step deeper into the mystery.

And then we are changed. These imprints of kinship are etched into us because they touch the soul. They are imprinted upon the body, upon the physical, the emotional, the psychic, and ultimately the spiritual self—because it is the soul that feels love in the deepest way. The language of love is the language of the soul. When the soul makes this intimate connection, kinship is truly rooted. Inner and outer are woven together.

In Sufism there is a saying: The seeker journeys from the world of visibility to the world of mystery. It begins with the body, with the beat of the heart, with physical sensation, with the phenomenal world. And where does that take you? Into places unknown, beyond the physical into the metaphysical. Time and place have that capacity. They are portals. They are magic. It is very important not to forget the earthly ties of kinship as we journey deeper into what might be called the soul or spirit realm, the transcendental realities so often severed from their origins. Many mystery schools veered away from the Earth, from Her, in pursuit of the timeless, of realms beyond the senses. But the deeper one moves into kinship—through place, through love—the further one descends into the depths of time, slipping closer to the timeless. And yet one must never forget where one has come from.

Too often those ancient ways of knowing were cut. The belief that what is above is better than what is below: It cuts. The simple reliance on a clock: It cuts. These wounds must be healed. The world must be braided back together, spirit and matter interwoven once more. Nothing can be excluded. Place cannot be excluded. Time cannot be excluded. She cannot be excluded.

If we wish to speak the language of love, then each interaction must be fresh—each time like the first, never tiring of it. When we walk through a landscape, whether familiar or new, we can step into a space of intimacy if we attend to the magic of how time lives within place. In this way, we begin to acknowledge and honor each place as a unique expression of Her love.

NINE

Remembering Earth Time

We cannot understand Earth Time through the lens of linear time. To do so risks intellectualizing an experience that must be lived. Instead we must relate to Earth Time through nonmental constructs: the body, the senses, our own cycles, and ultimately the heart.

Earth Time moves and functions like emptiness and form, and at the core of emptiness and form is love, the axis of all things. This may seem abstract, but if you are familiar with the concept, perhaps it is not. In essence, emptiness is the space that remains when the self, the ego construct, is removed, allowing the true nature of things to become apparent. It is the interconnected, interdependent nature of life, expressed both physically and metaphysically. Form is the way this appears—it is the tree outside the window, the self we inhabit, the material world we move through. When we strip away the construct of the ego self, what is revealed is relationship, an expanded sense of being not bound in duality but able to perceive the multiplicity and diversity within the Oneness of Being.

What holds the fabric of this interconnected, interdependent reality together? The Daoists would call it the Dao, or the Way. In Sufism we call it love. This is how I understand Earth Time. It is expressed in many ways, moving through life in shifting forms yet always holding emptiness at its center. And at the heart of that emptiness there is love. If we can tap into that aspect of ourselves, then a real connection with the Earth and all the forms She takes becomes possible. If we can return to this essence and consciously engage with Earth Time through the experience and language of love, we will begin to break free from the prison of linear time. In doing so, we build relationships rooted in something real.

When I say *something real*, I ultimately think of love. But you may think of it as energy—undiluted, unbroken, the essence of who we are, and the essence of all things. This essence exists in nonhuman forms that are free of ego. It is present in all that surrounds us. We don't need to create this relational way of being that allows us to see and engage with what is real. Rather, we must remove the constructs that obscure it: self, linear time, and ego. We do this by reconnecting to what is already speaking to us through the senses, the body, the cycles that exist within us, and finally the heart. When cultivated through practice, these relationships leave an imprint. They create a bond. And over time that bond deepens into an unbreakable form of kinship that honors the primordial covenant of relationship between us and the living Earth.

Kinship is not formed in a single moment but through returning again and again to the bond, building the relationship over time. This is how human bonds are developed. Each time we return, an imprint is left, and with every imprint the bond deepens. This bond not only fosters kinship but also weaves us into place, grounding us in relationship with the land itself.

For too long we have remained at a distance, looking but not engaging, or worse, looking away, seeing only ourselves. Trying to create a relationship is not yet participation; it is an approach, an effort, a reaching toward. But when these bonds take root, when these ties of kinship are lasting, we move from observing Earth Time to participating in it.

This participation is a form of communion with the living Earth. When we engage in this relationship rather than merely witnessing it or flirting with it, this communion begins to unfold in a process that deepens over time.

There is a distinction between connection and communion. Connection is like a kiss. Communion is a much deeper exchange of intimacy, where there is an experience of union, where we merge in the greater exchange that is unfolding all around us, where we shift from *I* to *we*. This experience of communion is also an act of healing and transformation, a way of being that reweaves the worlds of spirit and matter, re-sacralizing the Earth.

This is the practice of spiritual ecology at its fullest. At its heart it is communion with Earth in all the forms that may take. This is inherently individual. Each person engages with a tree, a river, a mountain, or a meadow differently because each of us is unique.

The danger of explaining concepts like Earth Time too concretely is that we begin to linearize the process. We make it mechanical, filtering the concept through what is familiar instead of letting go of habitual patterns and approaching it like a beginner encountering something for the first time, as a child in a state of wonder, or as one who enters stillness, where unknowing is its own form of understanding. Deliberately speaking abstractly is part of a much older tradition, one that exists within my own lineage but is also deeply rooted in Indigenous wisdom traditions, where speech moves in circles without a clear beginning or end. This way of speaking does not seek to define but to allow. As a culture we are addicted to knowing things with our rational mind. Even in seeking to create change or deepen a connection, we often rely on the familiar, on the intellect, and on a modern, Western rational way of thinking. But the art of speaking abstractly is still alive in many traditions. It is simply no longer alive in our culture.

We often think of ecology through a scientific lens, and that is valid. Yet too often this reduces the marvels of our living Earth to inanimate matter devoid of spirit and meaning. But what is matter without spirit? It is lifeless, devoid of light, devoid of love.

This spirit is a mystery. And if something is a mystery, it is too vast to fully comprehend. Climate change, for example, is too vast to grasp directly. But when we see it as a black hole—pulling everything in, unknowable—its presence starts to reveal itself to us at the edges. We can observe the ways it shapes what surrounds it. In doing so, we begin to perceive its contours without being consumed by it.

While this metaphor of a black hole is useful in describing the overwhelming and destructive nature of climate change, it can also apply to how we relate to forms beyond our comprehension—like a tree or the living world itself. We cannot come to know a tree by becoming it, but we can place ourselves in relation to it, looking not through a lens that separates but through one that acknowledges our shared reality. This is where practice comes in. Simply slowing the mind, we allow what is already within us to rise to the surface, opening us to another way of seeing.

We are not just our minds, our conditioning, or our inherited cultural way of being. Beneath all of that we are something else entirely. And while we are different from a tree, there is a shared language between us, just as there is a shared language between us and every other form around us. That shared language, for me, is the foundation of all things, the axis of all things: love, which is the meeting point of form and emptiness, the force that connects spirit and matter.

But when we separate ourselves and say, *That is a tree*, we are looking at a piece of matter from the outside. Even if we admire it, even if we call it sacred, it means nothing. We try to put words to it, but in the end it is not something to be explained. It is something to be lived. The truth is, as much as we have tried to speak about love over the centuries and millennia, it remains elusive; it is still a mystery.

We cannot change the world through a mental construct, through words alone. But words rooted in experience, as the poets of old discovered, have weight, which is why the role of story, and the storyteller, is so important. Story can contain the unseen thread, the spirit, that weaves through all things. As we try to understand and respond to the crisis around us, we must also look at what has been missing. And what is missing is love, spirit, and beauty. It is absent from the language of our governments, from the language of economists, from the language of social change and ecological five-point plans. It shouldn't be. Maybe in time that will change.

This language of love is the key. Just as there are many ways to experience love in human form, each person has their own experience of love with the more-than-human world, with our four-legged and winged kin. The language of love is unique, yet it is one the tree understands because it is the foundation of all things. I return to these points again and again as a method. To speak around something, to return to it from different angles, is a way of allowing its meaning to seep in. This way of speaking is less a linear progression with a beginning, middle, and end, than an incantation—a way of reminding, of opening. And it is in this way that we begin to move from observer to participant, from connection to communion.

Abstraction can lead to discomfort, but that's not a bad thing. For thousands of years Buddhists have expressed emptiness as form, just as Daoists and Zen practitioners have. How did they do it? Through the koan, through the poem, through the landscape painting. This is done so that you are taken into a space where discovery happens on its own. It must be discovered, not given. If we are told what it is, then it remains a construct. But if we are shown rather than told, we are drawn into a relationship.

No one likes being told who they are by someone else. It grows old fast. And yet our culture does it constantly. It doesn't just tell us who we are; it tells us what to buy, what to believe. It tells us everything. But the crisis we are facing is not just ecological or spiritual. It's a polycrisis, a crisis on every level. Everything must be reexamined. Everything must be overturned—including the most basic ways we define ourselves and our relationships.

For me, spiritual ecology is a way of life, an ongoing practice of learning how to be in relationship with the Earth from the most authentic part of oneself and expanding that understanding. For too long spiritual traditions have centered the transcendent, often speaking of universal truths while leaving the Earth out. The Golden Rule—*do unto others as you would have them do unto you*—was often repeated yet rarely extended to the more-than-human world. Not all traditions ignored the Earth, but many did and this became dangerous. These essential truths were turned into tools of power and control, placing the human at the center. They became unmoored, severed from their roots.

Now, we must extend our awareness to embrace the Earth with humility. Because even if we have always been drawn to reconnect on a deep level, we have also been complicit in ignoring the Earth as well—some of us more than others, depending on where we come from, what our ancestry holds, and what we have participated in. Humility is essential. We are beginners again. Yes, this ancient knowing is there, buried deep inside us, but we are relearning, and the posture of a learner is different from one who believes they already know.

We will make mistakes. As much as our best intentions might guide us, we will go out into the forest or onto a mountaintop and make it about ourselves. We will think, *That was a great experience for me.* Because it is hard not to. Remembering something as simple as the sacred nature of creation, and what that truly means, what it asks of us, is not easy. To hold a constant awareness of something at the center of all things, to relate to the world from that axis without letting it slip from consciousness—*that* is even harder. Maybe we will never fully get there, but we can try.

The world is changing on its own, unfolding along its own course. Yes, we have set things in motion. Science has given us a clear picture, its conclusions are irrefutable. But what comes to be, we will have to see. The details may shift—how much the sea will rise, how hot it will get, how many species will be lost are unknown—but the story is already in motion. Some things are still within our power. We could keep the oil in the ground—that would slow the damage, shift the trajectory. But the world is changing. The story is already being told.

What interests me most is the power of individual transformation, not for its own sake but for the sake of the whole. Yes, this can ripple into external change, but at its core it is about what becomes possible when we shift our awareness, our practice, our way of being to include the living Earth as part of who we are. As things fall apart in the coming years, the value of this inner transformation will be paramount. The keys that will unlock the doors to the world that might emerge in the coming decades or centuries will not be stored on a server. They will not live on a hard drive. Hard drives from ten years ago are already obsolete. Server farms, too, will vanish sooner than we think. How will the knowledge needed to keep a thread alive, to carry us through the liminal space between the end of one world and the beginning of another, endure? It will live within the human being and in community, within human beings in relationship with one another and Her. I believe it will be small because what is small is harder to corrupt. Large systems, even with the best intentions, are almost inevitably swallowed by the forces of greed, extraction, and desacralization. It is nearly impossible for them not to be. But small, contained communities and individual human beings hold something different. The human heart is far more difficult to corrupt. It can be corrupted, but not as easily as a system built on exploitation.

We, as individuals, as human hearts, as spiritual hearts, can be like time capsules, holding something inside us as we deepen into it—not as a tool but as a way of keeping something alive. This process of returning to the essential nature of all things—learning to speak the language of love in its essence, reorienting ourselves to the cycles of life, understanding time in a broader way and allowing that to change us—reshapes who we are. Not just mentally, though it does that too, but at the deepest levels of being. Like any real experience, when we allow it to filter up, it changes how we think. It comes from somewhere real inside of us. These seeds within us, these ways of being, can take root in how we live as human beings and societies.

We are part of this unfolding. Within us is the capacity to hold this essential truth, to carry these seeds, and to find ways to plant them. I return to the metaphor of seeds because they contain a whole blueprint for what will emerge even if it remains unseen for decades or longer. We speak of cathedral thinking, a way of imagining beyond our lifetime, and the many forms of future-oriented vision that we need, but if that thinking is not rooted in something real, it becomes just another concept. When we are truly rooted in what is real—this connection of love, the axis of all things, this relationship with the world as animate, alive, and sacred—then almost every act naturally aligns with that way of being.

An example of this is seventh-generational thinking, a Haudenosaunee principle that ensures that decisions made serve seven generations ahead of you, honoring living relationships over time.[10] This thinking emerged long ago as a natural extension of a way of being, one that may have taken shape gradually yet was always rooted in reality. Real change begins there. What follows is merely a reflection of that foundation, taking different external forms. That is what makes it beautiful: It is individual. Not something devised, but something lived. Cathedral thinking and seventh-generational thinking offer a broad frame that is adaptable in many ways. But this expanded vision must be grounded in what is real, in something lived, not merely conceived.

There is another dimension to this, perhaps the most esoteric of all. We tend to think that learning a way of being, a system of knowledge, means passing it on—teaching others, creating a ripple effect, generating change. This is true, but there is also a much older and esoteric form of transferring knowledge. When a human heart, when a human being, holds the knowledge of how to be in relationship with a broader reality, like remembering Earth Time, that knowledge can be made available to others through an inner space. One gains access to this inner space not through wireless networks or fiber-optic cables, or other modern forms of technological connection, but through the spirit threads that connect a human heart to other forms of reality.

When a person has outgrown the limitations of a single reality like a framework of time, they begin to seek what lies beyond. And at that moment a different form of time and its connected reality can be accessed. Something in you comes to an end and you can gain access to what lies beyond. One reaches a threshold and crosses it. If that knowledge is held and alive, you can gain access to that knowledge inwardly.

But what happens when such knowledge is no longer present? We often fail to grasp the true cost of what is being lost today. Take language, for example. Many of the world's remaining languages are spoken by only a small number of people. With each language that disappears an entire way of being in relationship to the place that language was developed disappears. A way of remembering Earth Time is erased. A language is not just words, it is a living system of knowledge. The names of plants, once sung into existence, fade. When a language dies, it is as if a light goes out. The people remain. They adapt. They change. But something vital is lost. If you ask them, they know this. The same is true of other ways of knowing. If these ways are alive within a human heart, within a community, they are like a note being sung. But what if one day no notes remain? What if whatever rises from the rubble has forgotten everything that came before?

This is why, traditionally, cultures like the Kogi of Colombia, who view themselves as the Elder Brothers, hold the knowledge of how to be in relationship with the Earth, including Earth Time. They understand their role as holding something consciously for the well-being of the world so that when someone needs it, it is there. And there are many ancient stories of this. Because if these systems of knowledge exist—not in textbooks, not on a website, not in a podcast or a video, but inwardly, within a human heart, within a lived system of knowledge—then they do not so easily disappear.

At this time, our responsibility is not primarily to seek personal spiritual salvation. It is to be of service, to hold something within our beings, within our hearts. Not as experts. Not as masters. We are not. There is a vast difference between our ability to carry a system of knowledge and the ability of those who came before us. But even if we fumble as we learn, even if our steps are uncertain, we have the capacity to walk this path. And perhaps a hundred or two hundred years from now these songs will still be there.

I am not the only one saying this. Many others, especially those within the very communities that have carried these systems of knowledge for thousands of years without corruption, have spoken of this. When you speak to elders from certain traditions, they will tell you, *We're just waiting it out for those in power to stop making a mess of it, and then we'll pick it up again.* But we have a role too. We must hold this in our hearts as best we can.

The beauty of it is that it changes you. This is not why we should do it, but it does. It has the capacity to fill you with love, to transform you. The way you relate to the world shifts. Often this comes with challenges, because letting go of familiar constructs and the systems we have relied on is never easy. This is why vulnerability matters. It draws you into a deeper space within yourself, and once you have tasted that, you do not want to go back. You want to live from that place. You want to honor it by allowing every interaction to reflect that part of yourself. In the end it is all so simple.

The challenge is holding on to this knowing in the midst of the noise, the rush of our lives, the city streets, the towers of industry surrounding us. How do we carry it with us? It cannot be something we practice only on a retreat; it must become part of our everyday life. She is limitless, and the opportunities to engage with Her are everywhere. We look up at the sky through the buildings. We may not see the stars, but She is still there.

If we integrate this knowing into our lives, if we move from observer to participant, if we aim for communion, we will remember. Even in the rush of the day—as we take our children to school and juggle meetings and work—we can find quiet moments in between to remember. When we pause, even for a breath, we will say: *I want to learn again how to be in relationship with You. I do not want to forget. I want again to remember how to be in relationship with You.*

TEN

Our Note

Remember me.

The Earth speaks first. Remembrance begins not with us, but with Her invitation. This is important for us to acknowledge. We are not inviting Her; rather, the Earth is always inviting us. It might come as a fleeting, faint whisper, barely audible—or as a roar:

Remember me!

This voice makes Herself known through awe, wonder, majesty, beauty, and magic. But also through pain, sorrow, grief, and suffering, almost asking the question:

Do you remember me?

And within that cry, imploring recognition, there is another:

What have you done?

We each have a unique heart that She calls upon. This is why the invitation, however we hear it, feels so potent. Because when someone speaks directly to your heart, your very soul, it feels intimate. It awakens something deep. *Remember me.* And if we have the courage to respond, to engage, to pick up that thread that was woven long ago into the fabric of our existence as human beings and say, *I remember you*, then a real practice of spiritual ecology begins. It's not words on a page, not a philosophy, not an intellectual concept, but something experiential.

We converse with Her as individuals. Even when we follow prescribed rituals, ceremonies, or practices, these do not dictate the experience itself, they simply *open* us. True ritual opens. Any real sacred act that is rooted in sincerity has the potential to open the heart. It can open the body. And the most powerful ones can even transform the mind. However it unfolds, this opening is always personal, always unique. And the response is just as individual, just as distinct. This exchange cannot be claimed by any single religion, spiritual tradition, or culture; it cannot be owned or controlled by anyone or any structure. This matters because it is also how existence itself functions. Each being in creation is like a node, bound to the source of its existence in this reality. Each holds a living connection that extends beyond itself, reaching toward something greater. Ownership by a single tradition is not part of this equation.

This is what was woven into our DNA: not just the memory of spirit and matter, not just the recognition that we *are* the Earth, but the remembrance of how this relationship is intimately experienced within each of us. When we begin to recognize this, the unique light within us begins to stir. It is as if we awaken within a vast forest network—a web of connections, nodes, and relationships, interwoven and dynamic, suddenly illuminated with spirit that moves through everything, animating what once seemed inert, revealing the deep intelligence that has always been there.

We are not just physical beings, just as She is not only a physical being. And we cannot remember Her in the same way anyone else does. Our individual offering of remembrance honors Her as the whole Earth, as a form of oneness, yet also honors the diverse expression of multiplicity. The field of existence is like that forest network—interwoven and dynamic. Each point of connection comes alive like a song that remembers Her in a way only we can. We each have a unique imprint of Her presence, carried within us and offered back, sewn into the fabric of creation.

When we as individuals enter this dance, this space, this relationship, we are engaging in an intimate knowing that demands to be lived. It becomes our responsibility to not only recognize this but to amplify it through an embodied practice that allows our individual note and offering to be expressed. In doing so all the other nodes that have awakened to their essential nature are supported. Like a Mother tree nourishing the other trees in the forest in need of water and nutrients, we nourish others purely by being in this embodied relationship and exchange with Her. When we let our note resound, we empower others to sing and offer their contribution, each as an individual spirit moving within the whole of creation, flowing in relationship with one another.

This is a practice not of learning, or even unlearning, but of *remembering.* It is also a practice of repetition, of attentiveness, of care. And, most important, of love. Because even when this ancient memory is awakened within us, obstacles arise. Even when something so true calls out—*remember me, remember me*—and our hearts come alive with recognition, Her voice can still be so easily muffled. Our human world does not want to remember Her. It is not easy. But what is worthwhile is never easy.

We might believe that this moment of awakening is the most powerful moment we can have when a whole new reality makes itself known. To awaken is to begin to see something as it really is, to hear the Earth as She calls your name through the breath of the wind or the cry of Her pain. But awakening is only the beginning of transformation. It is the first step where one crosses the threshold. The transformation continues to unfold through the steady rhythm of showing up, day after day. This is what makes it a practice, and ultimately, if one remains attentive and attuned, an embodied way of being. It requires our whole self so that the love awakened in our hearts grows from a nascent spark to a steady flame until She, this living Earth, becomes a constant presence inside of us.

Then we begin to hear those whispers everywhere. In the wind. In the water. In the silence between our footsteps. And those whispers become voices, become songs, and a veil of separation is lifted. Remembrance deepens through the simple, steady acts of greeting and honoring Her each day, just as the sun rises and the sun sets. Love moves like a spiral, drawing us deeper and deeper into the core of our being, and the core of Her being, until it is a constant presence. But we must have courage and persistence. Even the best intentions can so easily go astray, and then we fall back asleep. And when we do, we stop hearing the whispers of remembrance, the voices and the song.

Yet when we go deeper on this journey, something interesting happens: We are more able to offer love, give attention, and practice remembrance. All offering—all prayer in its essence—is a form of remembrance, whether we are offering thanks, asking for guidance, or simply acknowledging the presence of something greater than ourselves. Our faith in this relationship, which is bound up in our offering and prayer, is itself an acknowledgment of the Divine in all their forms and is a vessel for remembrance.

Remember me. I remember you. This exchange is the affirmation at the heart of existence that opens the door to union and, finally, communion. And just as no two voices sing the same song to Her, no two prayers are the same. Each is an intimate conversation, a relationship unlike any other. This is my favorite way to describe prayer: an intimate conversation. It is a secret language spoken between a soul and the Divine in all their forms—from crying out directly to the mysterious source of creation that is the Beloved to quietly praising Earth and Her endlessly generous embrace.

A story I often return to that reveals the nature of this intimate conversation is the one about the tenth-century Sufi mystic Dhūl-Nūn al-Miṣrī. The more fully he entered prayer, the more the Divine revealed its manifestations in the world to him. As his remembrance of God deepened, so did his ability to hear the Divine speaking:

> Whoever recollects God in reality, forgets all else besides Him, because all the creatures recollect Him, as is witnessed by those who experience a revelation (*kasht*). I experienced this state from evening prayer until one third of the night was over, and I heard the voices of the creatures in the praise of God, with elevated voices so that I feared for my mind. I heard the fishes who said: Praised be the King, the Most Holy, the Lord.[11]

He heard the distinct ways the Divine expresses itself through the voices of Earth's many creatures. He also understood that the nature of this relationship is not a one-sided conversation but inherently reciprocal. Giving and receiving move together in a fluid exchange. The more we offer, the more love expands within us. And as love expands within us, so does our ability to hear the myriad voices of the living Earth that always surround us.

This relationship is not static, but moves in a continuous, living exchange. When it is present and intact, something shifts and a different quality of being emerges. A resonance arises that was not there before as your note is met by Hers. Your song and Her song begin to coexist. This is where connection deepens, where what was fleeting becomes integrated. This is what is asked of us in this time: not merely to offer a momentary connection but to enter fully into communion, committing not for our sake but for Hers.

The Earth moves through rhythms of reciprocity and exchange, and what is true in the physical world is no different than in the world of spirit. If spirit and matter are to be reunited, we must return to this understanding. We must find the courage to stand in the midst of a culture that only takes, one that does not know the word *enough*, and offer ourselves. And there are so many ways to offer, both outwardly and inwardly. Just as with prayer and praise, the forms of offering are endless. And when we make an offering, it must come from the part of us that has been opened by love. For it is through the exchange of love that spirit and matter truly come together. When our spiritual nature encounters the spiritual nature of the Earth—at once whole and a multiplicity—a movement begins. Worlds are woven together, and what was static begins to flow.

The crisis we are experiencing is not about finding a solution but about returning to a fundamental truth: We are being asked to root ourselves once more in the most foundational essence of existence, a shared relationship of spirit, grounded in love that unites us. If we are to face what is unfolding, this must be restored. We are also being asked to recognize our great responsibility at this moment in time. It is not abstract or distant, but immediate and pressing. It is a responsibility to acknowledge Her presence and to respond, not only in special moments of reverence but through the constancy of our offering, through the daily act of commitment, whether or not we feel ready or even overwhelmed by the notion of this responsibility. For She does not pause to consider how She feels. She gives without ceasing. If we are to honor the reciprocal nature of existence, then we too must learn to do the same.

From this foundation anything can be built. This is why, across the world, systems of practice and protocol were developed to ensure that prayers and offerings were made, no matter the day, the season, or the circumstance. These systems made certain that the foundation would never be lost, that this elemental understanding of relationship would not disappear. But we cannot go back. If you are part of a culture that holds an intact tradition, one that has preserved the knowledge of living in relationship with the sacred and has kept systems, protocols, and practices to honor that balance, then you have the right to participate in it. But if you are not, you must either be formally invited into that tradition or find another way. Otherwise we co-opt intact systems of knowledge without real understanding or respect for the broader culture, cosmology, and ontology that the tradition sits within. The dark side of New Age culture has become extractive, where ceremonies like smudging and the reciting of certain prayers are often practiced without any real understanding or training in how to conduct those offerings. Instead, a different way will have to emerge that arises through individual commitment and takes form within both existing models and entirely new expressions.

I believe the future will reveal a path for cultures that have forgotten this fundamental truth, guiding them toward a way of being in relationship that can hold the sacred as it needs to be held. Because this relationship, this coming into a space of knowing the Divine, is deeply personal, it belongs to each of us in a way that no system can fully contain. I am a Sufi, and so I engage in this relationship primarily through the *dhikr*, the constant practice of remembrance of God interwoven with the breath but truly offered from the heart. But one does not need to be a Sufi, a Buddhist, a Christian, or to belong to any tradition at all. This knowing transcends form. Whatever structures emerge, whatever new practices and protocols come into existence, they must come from a recognition of the universality of this call while honoring the particular ways it moves through each of us. How these practices will arise, how they will take root in a world that has forgotten, is a question I continue to hold.

Until that unfolds, those of us who have awakened to the reality of this world, who have witnessed its severance from the sacred, and who have heard Her voice, or ache to hear it, bear a responsibility. We cannot wait for established systems to grant us entry, nor can we delay our participation until new traditions emerge to shape it for us. If a bridge is to span the space between now and what comes next, we must be the ones to lay its foundation.

A heart that has awakened to the nature of existence, to the living Earth and our place within Her, carries something rare and potent. This remembrance, when fully alive, does not linger as a distant echo of something lost but takes root in the body's knowing, becoming fully present and conscious. It is not a fragile or dormant memory but a force moving through one's being, shaping the way one sees, walks, speaks, and acts. And in that transformation each person becomes a point of light in the darkness of these times.

This is a radical act: To commit to a relationship, not for personal fulfillment, not as a means of spiritual comfort or a path to enlightenment, but for Her—for the Earth Herself, for the living intelligence that has been ignored for too long. To hold this remembrance in a world where there is no reflection of it—where the dominant culture denies its existence, where towers of industry, capitalism, and greed rise so high they block out the sun—is to be a sanctuary, a place where something essential is protected. To remember Her when all around us is forgetfulness. To cultivate this practice until it is no longer fleeting or theoretical but something lived, something embodied. To carry this relationship forward, not in defiance of the world as it is but as an affirmation of the world as it truly is and as it must be for the future.

An affirmation of the spirit imbued in all things.

An affirmation of our intimate relationship with our home, with our source.

An affirmation of what it means to be human.

ELEVEN

Prayer, Spirit, and Matter

Now in this moment in our history we are being called to return to a deep memory, to recover something long buried. There is a circular relationship unfolding, requiring us to look back in order to move forward. To remember what we once knew—that the Earth is a sacred being. The arc of our evolution led us into new forms of knowledge, and yet in striving for more we lost something vital; we became unmoored from what it really means to be human. This call to remembrance is both a response to the urgency of the present crises and an acknowledgment of something deeper. This memory is not merely recollection; it is a reality. It is a part of our being, just as it is a part of the Earth's being. And in truth, they are one and the same.

This is more than a return. It is part of a larger evolutionary unfolding that will continue long after our lifetimes. It is part of the healing that must take place on this planet. It is the next step in our relationship, not only with the Earth as we know it but with the Earth as a divine being. What was once whole, our relationship with the sacred, has been fractured. Now we must heal and mend this split.

We can begin by returning to a way of communion. Prayer is one of the most fundamental ways of practicing communion and engaging with the sacred nature of creation. Prayer is a space one enters, a state of being. It may begin in silence, form into words, and then, ultimately, be offered through the heart. Over time it expands beyond the self, becoming an experience of prayer that surrounds you— an atmosphere, a way of walking in the world. The Divine in all Their forms is no longer distant but ever present. In this exchange—looking toward the Earth that holds us and finding that the Earth is gazing back—the distance dissolves.

There is an urgent need to recognize the Divine presence in the living world and to integrate this awareness into our prayers. The Earth, this vast and ancient being, is not separate from the sacred but a revelation of it. To pray with and for the Earth is to acknowledge Her suffering, to reweave the threads of relationship that have been severed. It is to remember that prayer is not only a reaching to a transcendent beyond but also a returning—to the ground beneath our feet, to the breath that moves through all things, to the reciprocity between spirit and matter.

Prayer with the Earth invites us not only to turn inward but to open ourselves to the living world, to recognize the sacred presence within the Earth and to embody this awareness. To pray in this way is to rekindle the reciprocity that has been forgotten. It is to remember that prayer is not only an ascent but a descent, an anchoring into the depths of the world, into the soil and stone, to feel the sacred pulse that moves through all things beneath us.

Through prayer we learn to see with the eye of the heart and in turn to attune to something greater than ourselves. It requires an act of remembering, a deeper stream of memory that is ancestral, collective, and woven into the very fabric of humanity's relationship with the Earth. It is waiting for us to find the thread again, to remember the role of prayer. When the heart turns, when prayers are offered and remembrance stirs within us, we are drawn back into that continuity. It rises to the surface, revealing the depth of our relationship with the Earth.

We are each unique, shaped by what we have lived, by the deep histories that move through us. As this memory rises, we slowly begin to see the value of our unique offering. With each step toward Her, our true essence emerges, calling out: *I am here for You.* This is the cry of something essential within us that has always known the way. Little by little, we remember where we have come from. Only then can we begin to see where we are going.

The memory of humanity's relationship with the divine being that is this Earth is as old as human life itself. It is not only a spiritual inheritance; it is a physical one, carried in the body, in the blood, in the collective experience of what it means to be human. It is the deep, ancient knowing that we belong to this Earth, that we arise from Her, formed from Her elements and sustained by Her breath.

Our forgetfulness of this lies at the heart of the crisis we now face. Every form of destruction we see around us can be traced back to this severance. Some spiritual paths once honored the sacred nature of creation—these were traditions that praised the Earth, worked with Her, and knew Her as a living presence. Others acknowledged this only in part or not at all. But whether this recognition feels familiar or distant does not matter. What matters is the act of awakening itself, for in that act we can step into an essential understanding needed in this time. This is not a sentimental notion but an evolutionary necessity. The trajectory of human life depends on it. What was cast aside, often for reasons of power or violence, must be surfaced, restored, and returned to its rightful place. And so we must uncover this memory within us: that we are part of Her.

For many, this memory awakens through a deep love and care for the Earth. Often this search is born from pain. The grief of witnessing the world unravel—cultures fraying, the more-than-human world pushed further and further away—can break something open. It is a wound that reveals, an ache that unlocks. Like a child torn from its mother, it is a grief that is met with grief, the mother crying for the child and the child crying for the mother. And when that pain stirs, something long buried rises to the surface. A doorway that was closed begins to open.

You feel it inside of you, tapping into something deeper than words can reach. We not only feel the weight of what is unfolding, we can begin to engage with it, stepping into a space that holds more than a personal longing for God or Truth or meaning. The moment one begins to remember, everything changes. A whole new set of possibilities emerges, not just for one's own journey but for perceiving and participating in the great unfolding.

There are two dreams I have had over the past decade related to the ancient nature of our relationship with the Earth that I find myself returning to again and again.

The first dream presented me with an image of a tower, an immense structure stretching from the ground into the heavens, so high that I could not see its top. The tower had many floors, like a great skyscraper, yet each level was distinct, shaped by its own character and design. It was ancient—immeasurably so. Very, very old.

Some floors bore carved statues reminiscent of the gargoyles perched on the edges of old cathedrals. Others were adorned with intricate patterns and inscriptions, their origins lost to time. The sheer diversity of forms was staggering, and the tower extended endlessly upward.

As I stood before it, I understood that each floor represented a cultural epoch unfolding from the beginning of human history. Each was built upon what had come before, forming a kind of evolutionary journey. And at the heart of this unfolding was a continuous thread that passed through the different ways that each culture, since time immemorial, had expressed its relationship to the Divine. That relationship was inscribed on every floor of the tower. Then my gaze was drawn downward toward the base of the tower. There stood four massive statues of ancient lions, their mouths gaping open. And from their open jaws a descent stretched down and down into darkness.

It became clear that every floor of the tower had been built upon this space, accessed through the lions' mouths. Every culture had emerged from those depths, rising from something far older than itself.

Then suddenly an explosion erupted. Fragments of rock shot out from the lions' mouths and the foundation that had supported all these cultures was destroyed. The feeling was overwhelming, almost indescribable. I thought: *Everything will fall. Everything will collapse.*

But it didn't. The tower wavered, teetering on the edge of ruin, yet it remained standing. And I understood—the structure that had been created through the unfolding of time was still holding itself together, but its foundation was gone. The root from which everything had arisen had been shattered. I was left with the question: *How much longer could this hold?*

And this is where we are now: this ancient root, upon which everything was built, now destroyed, whether in part or in full, by what we have done to Her.

The second dream was different, but deeply connected. The dreams shared the same aesthetic, as if painted by the same unseen hand, though years had passed between them.

In this second dream, a great scroll unfurled before me. At its top lay the surface of the Earth. It was as if I were seeing a cross section of a piece of land, as though someone had cut through it, revealing everything from the surface to the deepest layers beneath.

As the scroll continued to unfold, it became clear that this was more than a landscape—it was a map. A map that tracked both place and time. At the very top, above the Earth, was our present moment in history. Just below, a small mark indicated the Romans. Further down, another mark read "Greeks" and then "Minoan." And below that, still more names—some familiar, others lost to time. Each civilization, each epoch, was pressed just beneath the surface, its presence still close.

The deeper the scroll went, the further back it reached into histories buried beneath memory.

Then, just two or three feet below the surface, the first roots appeared. As the scroll continued to unfurl, more roots emerged—layer upon layer, interwoven, descending deep into the depths of time. They reached further and further down, revealing a vast, intricate network. It became clear: These roots represented humanity as it had evolved over tens of thousands of years.

At the very top, in a thin layer of strata just beneath the surface, lay the so-called great civilizations of antiquity. And yet, unlike us, they remained connected to the Earth, still rooted beneath the surface. They had not severed their ties to the living world. They were part of the same story as the first dream, the story of how ancient, how foundational our relationship with the Earth truly is.

This memory that we carry is like that. It reaches further back than what we think of as history to a time when we all shared a primordial covenant of relationship with the Earth. When it surfaces, whether it arises naturally or is awakened through a conscious turning of attention, it must be nurtured so that it is not forgotten. Otherwise it is easily obscured. The world veils it—the ego, distractions, the ten thousand things that pull us away from what is most true in ourselves. There must be attention given. There must be recognition. One way to tend to this ancient, latent memory within us is through prayer. Since the dawn of existence this memory has been sustained through prayer and praise offered in a myriad of forms. In the dream, the inscriptions on every floor of the tower, rising toward the heavens, were a reflection of the many ways in which cultures have acknowledged the sacred nature of creation, the divine being that is the Earth. Prayer took many forms: song, ceremony, dance, silence, incantation—each a unique expression of devotion.

Part of what allowed the great forgetting—the desacralization of the world—was the silencing of these forms of prayer, for prayer and praise helped hold the worlds of spirit and matter together. They were a kind of magic. If we are to keep this recognition of who She is alive, we must give our attention; we must offer our recognition. And we can do this through prayer, through praise. That is part of what we are being called to now.

We are not strangers to praise and prayer. It is what we drink when we are thirsty. It is what already sustains so many of us, regardless of what faith or tradition we come from. It is what we eat when we are hungry. It is what puts us to sleep at night and wakes us in the morning. And as we make this journey back to remembrance, we become more and more familiar with our own unique way of offering ourselves, with our own imprint of devotion. Our voice grows stronger, our heart beats louder, and our blood moves with greater force through our veins. Our capacity to praise expands because we have made space within ourselves for it. And as that space widens, our ability to praise deepens.

We must turn our attention toward Her. And as we do, this remembrance should grow, should deepen, until it becomes part of every breath. The more one remembers, the greater the heart's capacity becomes. The Sufis say the heart is the vastest thing in existence, with the capacity to hold not only all the seen and unseen worlds but the entirety of the Earth and the universe itself. In the past one had to embark on a long journey to arrive at this knowledge, and hidden mystical secrets were known only to initiates. But access to this dimension of the heart has changed because the need has changed. The cry of the Earth has opened the heart, and now one can experience and participate in this ancient exchange regardless of where one is on their spiritual journey. If the heart is open, it is enough. To keep this memory alive within us is all that is asked—to offer the recognition and honoring that is needed, to help at a time when our help is needed.

I believe the only way we will find our way through this unraveling is through the braiding together of spirit and matter. And this braiding is at the heart of prayer. But we can no longer relate to matter as something dead or inert. We must relate to matter as a divine form, as sacred. In each form that matter takes there is a divine presence. The Earth as a divine being is present in these forms, and where She comes from is present. The energy behind creation is *in* creation. And part of the mystical secret is learning how to be present with the Divine in all their forms, including Her. And when one prays, not only through the utterance or words or the silent recollection in one's heart but with eyes wide open, walking in remembrance—looking, hearing, seeing, perceiving—one is offering praise. Because in that state one's heart is attuned to all the physical forms of the Divine that She embodies. And when this happens, when spirit meets matter, spirit also meets spirit. Our spirit, our light, engages with Her spirit and Her light, the light within matter, the light within us. This in turn honors something central to the human experience that we have long forgotten: that we are sacred, that we are divine. And through this recognition, something is also stitched back together that has been severed.

The foundation of our existence has been ruptured by our actions, and so we must heal that wound. This weaving of spirit and matter unfolds through our practices of remembrance, and it is a lifelong commitment because the wound is deep, the wound is old. Will we see its healing in our own lifetimes? I think it is doubtful. Maybe glimpses, if we are fortunate. Maybe pieces. And yet if we are here for something greater than ourselves, if we wish to honor the Divine and honor the Earth for Her sake, then it matters not what we get to experience in this life. What matters is what we do in each moment, because of the responsibility we carry. When we have been awakened to the reality of existence, not just existence in some broad metaphysical sense but existence as it is unfolding now, in this moment of history, it becomes our duty to remember. We have to. Once something has been awakened, it must be remembered. Just as when the heart is stirred from its sleep, it must be remembered and remembered again.

In the Qur'ān it is written, "Am I not your Lord? Yes, we witness it" (Surah Al-A'raf–7:172). This acknowledgment of our relationship with the Divine as lord and creator is for the Sufi at its heart a love affair between lover and Beloved. But how can we embrace one aspect of our Beloved and ignore another when in truth they are the same Beloved? She is part of our Beloved, and acknowledging this is part of returning to what it means to be in relationship with the Divine in all Their forms. This primordial covenant of relationship is multifaceted. We witness it in so many ways. The transcendent Beloved and the immanent Beloved walking hand in hand. And so we praise and we pray to the Divine in unlimited ways, and as we do, we weave the worlds back together.

Sufis call themselves weavers, weaving the divine substance of love so that it flows between the worlds. But one does not need to be a Sufi to participate in this work. This work belongs to those of every faith and tradition and to those who claim none. It is for lovers of the Earth, for those who are drawn to work with love, the divine substance that encases the heart and is capable of transforming one's whole being. This memory awakens a love that is deep and very old. Our prayers are filled with this love. Our bodies are filled with this love. Our eyes are filled with this love. And so we praise, one stitch at a time and one prayer at a time. And we help to weave the worlds back together.

Our prayers can bridge the worlds—creation and Creator, spirit and matter. And if we ignore this, we are not just ignoring the need at this time, we are ignoring our origins. So we pray. We praise. We remember. We honor the Divine and we honor Her. And we do it for the rest of our lives. We focus less on the result and more on the offering, as that is our contribution. The love. The prayer. The honoring of who we really are. The Divine in all Their forms. This is our story.

PART TWO

EMBODIMENT

PRACTICES

The following practices focus on what is most essential and fundamental—the breath, the heart, walking, listening, and time—and are intended to offer ways to begin embodying a spiritual ecology. The breath and heart practices especially serve as a foundation for the others. They draw directly from key methods and techniques within my own Sufi path and are designed to work with the power and presence in the breath and the energy of love within the heart. These spiritual technologies are truly universal in nature and are found in numerous spiritual traditions.

I recommend doing these practices sequentially to start, as they build on one another, gradually integrating components from each one. After experimenting with them all, I encourage you to create your own sequence or way of practicing with them, experiencing how they interrelate. You could go on a daylong hike, beginning with the walking and breathing with the Earth practice and stopping after an hour or two to sit next to a rooted being and engage with Kinship Time. As you continue to walk, you could practice observing the cycles in a landscape, until you pause again to listen to the winds, or to the water of a river or stream you come across. Then spend a half hour resting in the shade practicing immersion in the heart meditation before walking into the evening light, offering prayers of gratitude to the Earth as you walk and take in Her beauty. But these practices don't require an idyllic setting and can just as easily be integrated into your daily routine as you walk to work or school, take a moment at lunch to step outside and listen to the wind and birdsong, and offer a silent prayer acknowledging the presence of Her voice amid the clamor of ours.

I see these practices as just a beginning, the foundation for an embodied spiritual ecology that can be applied to and integrated into many aspects of our lives: cooking, gardening, growing and eating food. Engaging all the senses in our relationship with Her, celebrating the extraordinary and the mundane, from gazing at the full moon on summer nights to raking leaves and composting our food. These are but a few examples.

These practices are simple and can be done for the rest of one's life. They are designed to open a connection with the living Earth or deepen one that already exists. Like the cycles they are built on, they interconnect and expand like a series of concentric circles. Over time, if you allow it, they can take you from a space of connection with the Earth toward a space of communion.

The following practices are available as guided audio experiences at https://www.shambhala.com/remembering-earth-practices. Before you begin, I recommend silencing your phone, or, better yet, if you are not using the audio, leaving it behind entirely. As these practices are primarily done outside, be smart and safe—if you're going to be gone for some time, consider telling someone where you're going and check in with them when you return.

TWELVE

Breath

Not Christian or Jew or Muslim, not Hindu,
Buddhist, sufi, or zen. Not any religion
or cultural system. I am not from the East
or the West, not out of the ocean or up
from the ground, not natural or ethereal, not
composed of elements at all. I do not exist,
am not an entity in this world or in the next,
did not descend from Adam and Eve or any
origin story. My place is placeless, a trace
of the traceless. Neither body or soul.
I belong to the beloved, have seen the two
worlds as one and that one call to and know,
first, last, outer, inner, only that
breath breathing human being.

    —RŪMĪ[12]

We take our first breath the moment we emerge into this world from our mother's womb and take our last before returning to our source. Breathing is our most primal and essential act. Simply put, to breathe is to live. Yet as primal and physical as breathing is, it is also so much more than that. Throughout different cultures the spirit or soul has long been thought to reside within the breath. The word *spirit* originates from the Latin *spiritus*, which means "breath." In ancient Greek the word for breath is *pneuma*, which also carries the meaning of spirit, soul, and even wind. In Hebrew the word *ruach* was used to describe breath, wind, and the spirit of God. In Sanskrit the word *prana*, the primal life force and energy that permeates everything in existence, is derived from the roots *pra-*, meaning "before, forward," and *-an*, meaning "to breathe and be alive," pointing to the flowing nature of this force. There are even five types of *pranas*, known as the *vāyus*, or "winds." And in ancient Chinese philosophy, breath is closely associated with *Qi*, which, like *prana,* is considered to be the vital energy that permeates the universe. Needless to say, this understanding is both rich and very old.

This relationship between breath and spirit was foundational to many of the spiritual practices that emerged in various traditions over the last few thousand years. It underlies the power of a mantra; it serves as a gateway to stilling the mind; and it can allow one to harness a flow of energy beyond oneself, as in the yogic practice of *pranayama*. In my own Naqshbandi Sufi tradition, awareness in the breath (*hush dar dam*) is the first of its eleven principles. It forms the foundation of the Sufi practice of dhikr, or remembrance of God, where the repetition of the name(s) of God is aligned with the breath. Baha ad-din Naqshband, the fourteenth-century Sufi saint for whom my tariqa is named, said: "The foundation of our work is in the breath. The more that one is able to be conscious of one's breathing, the stronger one's inner life."[13]

Many meditation practices—from Vipassana and mindfulness to Zen—begin with focusing on the breath to cultivate awareness in the present moment and clear the mind. Just by following the cycle of the in-breath and out-breath one can begin to slow down one's thoughts, calm one's emotions, be present in the moment, and be more aware of our surroundings. I find that being aware of one's breath is a simple and effective way to prepare oneself to engage directly with the living world—not absorbed in our mind but rooted in our body, attentive to the more-than-human world that constantly surrounds us. It helps create the right conditions and space for a connection with what lies beyond the self. Practiced over time, it can lead to a quality of porousness that opens a door to a deeper communion with the Earth.

Becoming aware of the breath also allows us to connect our own essential nature with the broader reality that surrounds us. In the Sufi tradition, it is taught that the soul or higher self enters the body with each out-breath and returns to its source and spiritual dimension with each in-breath. Awareness of the space between the inhalation and the exhalation is given utmost importance, as the presence of one's higher consciousness resides there and can then be directed to flow into the body, and, in turn, into the phenomenal world. The cycle of breath then becomes a cycle of prayer, the out-breath offering our most essential self to the world of creation, the in-breath, carrying the life force and spirit present within creation, offered back to its source.

Within this world of creation, our breath participates in a continuous exchange with the more-than-human world. Like us, all animals breathe in oxygen and breathe out carbon dioxide. The oxygen we breathe is primarily generated by the process of photosynthesis as plants and trees on land and phytoplankton in the ocean turn sunlight and carbon dioxide into the air we breathe. We share breath with the plants, trees, oceans, myriad creatures, and even starlight, all participating in a cycle of reciprocity that forms the foundation for all life within this living, breathing Earth.

The breath lies at the heart of all these relationships, inner and outer; it is a shared exchange of the essential building blocks of life and, most important, the relationship between spirit and matter. For within each inhalation and exhalation the spirit that underlies creation, that flows into matter and bridges the worlds, is present.

Our offering of remembrance begins with the breath.

The following three breath practices build on each other, incorporating new elements as they unfold. I suggest moving through them sequentially to start, until you are familiar with them.

I

AWARENESS OF THE MOMENT

Approx. 30 minutes

Find a quiet spot, preferably outdoors, where you won't be disturbed. Sit in any position that allows you to relax comfortably for a while.

Close your eyes and put your attention on your breath. Breathe slowly and naturally. Breathe in through your nose, noticing that as you do your belly expands. Breathe out through your mouth, letting your belly release.

Continue for a few minutes.

Feel the expansive field of space and energy that enters your body with each in-breath and the tension, stress, and smallness of the body and the self that is released with each out-breath. Allow yourself to expand into the space that the cycle of the breath creates.

As thoughts arise, don't fight or engage with them, just return to the breath, focusing all your attention on the in-breath, the space at the top of the in-breath, and the out-breath.

Continue for 20–25 minutes,
or for longer if you'd like.

When you feel ready, gently open your eyes and take in the world around you before you get up and go about your day.

You will find that this simple practice can quickly bring you into a different state of awareness, one that isn't caught in the chatter of the mind, the endless to-do lists, the replaying of what happened yesterday, or wondering what could happen tomorrow. Through doing this practice you will become more present in what is unfolding around you: the wind on your face, the sounds of distant voices, birdsong filling the air.

Over time, this practice will heighten your awareness, allowing you to learn to just be more present in the moment.

II

BREATHING FROM OUR ESSENCE

Approx. 30 minutes

Find a quiet spot, preferably outdoors, where you won't be disturbed. Sit in any position that allows you to relax comfortably for a while.

Starting with the out-breath, breathe slowly and deeply, allowing the body to relax, the mind to settle.

After a few minutes, place your attention on the space at the top of the inhale before you begin to exhale, noticing that you naturally pause here. The pause may be brief or it might last for several seconds. Continue for several cycles, keeping your attention focused on this space between the in- and out-breath.

On the out-breath, visualize the breath as energy flowing from this space at the top of the inhale into the body, and then outward into the space surrounding you—the air, the ground beneath your feet, the nearby plants and trees. On the in-breath, visualize the air you breathe as energy entering the body and flowing upward toward the head and the top of the inhale. As the in-breath crests, visualize the energy brought into the body being absorbed into the vastness that exists there.

*Continue this for several minutes until
you feel a sense of expansion.*

Now, as you breathe out, hold in your consciousness this intention: *I offer my essential nature to you.* Feel your breath flowing into the air around as an offering of energy. And on the in-breath hold this intention: *My essential nature is nourished by you.* Feel the nourishment offered through the air and energy you breathe as it is absorbed into the vastness of the Self.

*Continue for 20 minutes,
or for longer if you'd like.*

When you feel ready, gently open your eyes and take in the world around you before you get up and go about your day.

Whether you think of our essential nature as a soul, spirit, divine essence, or none of these doesn't really matter. What matters is that you offer what feels most essential to your nature as you breathe from the depths of yourself, that you begin to feel there is an energy within the breath that can be offered to the space that surrounds you as you breathe out, and that you receive and are nourished by an energy from this space with each in-breath, stepping toward a space of reciprocity with the living world.

III

SHARED BREATH

Approx. 30 minutes

Find a quiet spot, preferably outdoors, where you won't be disturbed. Sit in any position that allows you to relax comfortably for a while.

Breathe slowly and deeply, focusing on the natural pause at the top of each inhale.

On the out-breath, imagine offering energy from your essence into the air around you, and on the in-breath, imagine receiving an offering of energy that nourishes your essence.

Focus on this cycle for a few minutes.

Now, on the out-breath, hold the awareness that what you are breathing out is carbon dioxide. Visualize it dispersing into the air, being absorbed by plants and trees and ocean. On your in-breath, hold the awareness that you are breathing in oxygen offered by these same plants, trees, and ocean.

Focus on this cycle for a few minutes.

Let go of the focus on the exchange of carbon dioxide and oxygen. Instead, visualize your out-breath as energy filling the air around you, then being absorbed by plants and trees and ocean as their in-breath. As you breathe in, visualize the breath offered by the plants, trees, and ocean entering your body as a life force, a gift from numerous living beings that nourishes you.

Focus on this cycle for a few minutes.

Now, expand your visualization to include animals, each one nourished by the breath of plants, trees, and ocean as you breathe in. Imagine your breath meeting and mingling with the breath of other living beings, all participating in a continuous exchange of shared breath—a gift of life, an energy of mutuality.

Focus on this cycle for a few minutes.

Expand your visualization even further to include the whole Earth, holding in your awareness how your breath contributes to the whole Earth and in turn how you are nourished by the whole Earth.

Focus on this cycle for a few minutes.

To end, visualize the Earth Herself breathing. Feel the ongoing cycle that has always existed, holding in your awareness how your breath meets Her breath, how we are part of a continuous cycle of shared breath. That this is what it means to be part of a living, breathing Earth.

When you feel ready, gently open your eyes and take in the world around you before you get up and go about your day.

THIRTEEN

Heart

I saw him on the streets of the hidden with something in his hand. I said, "My God, what is this?" He said, "Your heart." I said, "Has my heart such a station that it lies in your hand?" He gazed at my heart, and it was like something folded up, so he spread it out. And my heart covered the space from the throne to the Earth. I said, "This is my heart?" He said, "This is your heart, and it is the vastest thing in existence." He took it, as it was still in his hand, to the angelic regions, and I went with him, until I reached the treasury of the hidden of the hidden. I said, "Where are you taking it?" And he said, "To the world of eternity, so that I may look in it, and create the wonders of reality in it, and forever manifest myself in it with the attribute of divinity."

—RUZBIHAN BAQLI[14]

Ask a Sufi about the heart and you might wish you hadn't, for we will no doubt go on and on; for us, the heart is everything. It is here that we seek refuge, because it is here that love resides. It is in the heart that the spark of Divine love, once awakened, grows into a flame—and ultimately into a fire of longing. The heart beckons us, holds us, and if we are lucky, sets us free. As the ninth-century Sufi saint and martyr Mansour al-Hallaj famously said, "When the Truth has taken hold of a heart, She empties it of all but Herself!"[15]

The mystics say we have two hearts, the physical one and the spiritual one. It is said that the spiritual heart lies just behind the physical heart and is a center of energy that can be accessed in numerous ways. In ancient India this was described in the Vedas and Upanishads as one of the seven *chakras*, or energy centers that exist along the spine, from the root chakra at the base of the spine to the crown chakra at the top of the head. In Sufi traditions chakras are known as *lataifs*, or subtle energy centers within the body that are seen as places of connection to the Divine.

For the Sufi, the spiritual heart is considered vast beyond comprehension, so vast that even the entire cosmos could become lost within it. As the great Sufi philosopher Ibn 'Arabi asks, "When the heart encompasses the Eternal, how can it possibly notice the existence of the temporary?"[16] This miraculous space within the human being is where the ego is drowned by love, where our self ultimately dissolves. It is where connection deepens into communion, where what once lay at the surface sinks into the depths. And perhaps most important: It is the conduit through which we offer ourselves to the Divine in all Their forms. Like the substance of love and the Divine source from which it flows, it is also deeply mysterious.

Yet as mysterious and abstract as a heart may be, it is also very much a tangible, physical organ, pumping blood through our bodies with each beat. Through it we feel our first loves, the joy of the birth of a child, the grief of a loved one's passing, and the many simple pleasures of life that touch the soul. These feelings aren't abstract, they are felt in the body, even in the bones. The love that flows through the mystical heart is felt within the physical one. And it is in both hearts that the primordial love we share with the Earth resides. For it is here that the inner meets the outer.

When the heart is activated, it opens a doorway between us and the Divine, becoming a bridge from the Creator, the source of divine love, to the world of creation. Across Sufi, Yogic, and Buddhist traditions, spiritual practices were developed to activate the energy center within the heart and to evoke, cultivate, and channel this love. Within my own Naqshbandi Sufi tradition, we practice a simple heart meditation to empty the mind and deepen into the heart, dissolving into the love that resides there. Over time this becomes a transformative practice where what is first felt inwardly in meditation becomes embodied and present in waking consciousness. Eventually love becomes a constant lived experience.

The following three practices are variations of the heart practice I have been doing since I was a child. They are intended to help awaken us to the mystery of the Divine in all Their forms and to deepen our love for the Earth and all the beings that exist within Her.

The practices build on each other, incorporating new elements as they unfold. I suggest moving through them sequentially to start, until you are familiar with them.

I

BREATHING WITH THE HEART

Approx. 30 minutes

Find a quiet spot, preferably outdoors, where you won't be disturbed. Sit in any position that allows you to relax and remain comfortable for the duration of the practice.

Close your eyes and put your attention on your heart. Feel it beating and how it lies at the center of your chest.

*Spend a few minutes being
with this sensation.*

Now begin to focus on your breath. Notice the out-breath, the in-breath, and the space at the top of the in-breath. After a few cycles, begin to visualize the breath as energy flowing from the space at the top of the in-breath into the heart on the exhale. Let it rest there for a couple of seconds and then breathe in, visualizing the breath rising as energy from the heart, moving up through the chest and neck and out of the top of the head, releasing into the space at the top of the inhale.

Stay with this cycle for a few minutes.

As you continue breathing and visualizing this cycle, you will begin to feel a subtle energetic expansion in the heart as it becomes infused by the energy of the breath. Place your conscious awareness on this feeling of expansion in the heart, continuing to breathe and visualize the flow of energy moving down into your heart and then up through the chest and neck to the top of your head.

Focus on this cycle for fifteen minutes,
or for longer if you'd like.

When you feel ready, gently open your eyes and take in the world around you before you get up and go about your day.

By placing your attention on the heart and breath and visualizing the energetic exchange present between them, you can begin to expand your heart. It becomes infused with the energy present in the breath, and by breathing from the space between the inhalation and the exhalation you bring the presence of your essential nature into the heart.

This is a simple but potent practice that can lead to both a deeper awareness of the heart and a felt sense of its expansive nature. I like to think of it as a little warm-up exercise to get the heart going and ready to be opened by love.

II

IMMERSION IN THE HEART

Approx. 30 minutes

Find a quiet spot, preferably outdoors, where you won't be disturbed. Sit in any position that allows you to relax and remain comfortable for the duration of the practice.

Close your eyes, put your attention on your heart, and focus on the breath. On the out-breath, visualize or sense energy flowing from the space at the top of the inhale down into the heart. On the in-breath, visualize or sense energy rising up through the chest and neck and then flowing out through the top of the head.

As you continue breathing and visualizing this cycle, you will begin to feel a subtle energetic expansion in the heart as it becomes infused by the energy of the breath. Place your conscious awareness on this feeling of expansion in the heart.

Continue with this cycle for a few minutes.

Once your heart is activated, think of someone you love. It could be a partner, a parent, a child—anyone who evokes a palpable sense of love in your heart when you think of them. It could also be a place or a pet. What matters is that a real sense of love exists between you and them. Focus on this felt sense of love.

With your attention focused on this love for this person, place, or animal, thoughts will naturally begin to arise that distract your focus. As the thoughts emerge, visualize placing them into your heart, immersing them in the love that is present there. Repeat this process over and over again, imagining each time that the thoughts are being drowned by the love in the heart.

If the mind becomes too active and the visualization of immersing your thoughts in the heart too challenging, simply return to the breath. Visualize the out-breath flowing into the heart and the in-breath flowing up the chest and neck and out of the top of the head and into the space between the inhalation and exhalation. Stay with this for a few minutes. Then return to visualizing the thoughts being drowned in the heart.

*Continue for 20 minutes, or
for longer if you'd like.*

When you feel ready, gently open your eyes and take in the world around you before you get up and go about your day.

While this is, in essence, a simple meditation practice, it can take time to feel a lasting presence of expanded love within the heart. Like all real meditation practices, you have to stick with it and return to it again and again. Over time the association between love and a particular person or place will fall away and you will find yourself simply able to feel a presence of love within the heart whenever you place your attention there. It is as if the connection between you and the one you love sparks a nascent flame that is always present in the heart, waiting for you to blow on it. Over time it may even become a fire.

This is a practice I have done for forty years and that has the potential to open one to the vastness within the heart.

III

PRESENCE OF THE HEART

Approx. 45 minutes

Go outside and find a place where the vibrancy of the living world feels close and tangible. If you live in an urban space, this could be a nearby park or green space, your garden, or even a balcony where you can see the sky.

Find a quiet spot where you won't be disturbed. Sit in any position that allows you to relax and remain comfortable for the duration of the practice. You may want to lean against a tree or lie in some soft grass.

Return to the immersion in the heart practice: Close your eyes, and with each out-breath sense energy flowing down into your heart, and with each in-breath sense energy rising up and out through the top of your head.

Think of a person, place, or animal you love, and focus on the feeling of love expanding your heart.

Continue for 20–25 minutes.

Slowly open your eyes and take a deep breath, adjusting to the light. With the feeling of love still palpable in your heart, take in your surroundings. With your eyes, acknowledge the plants, trees, grass, soil, and other living beings around you, holding the intention in your heart: *I see you*. With your ears, listen for the wind in the rustling of branches and leaves, the buzzing of insects, the calls of birds, or the sounds of nearby human voices, holding the intention in your heart: *I hear you.*

Continue for 5–10 minutes.

Return your focus to your breath. As you breathe out, visualize your breath as an energy of love flowing outward from your heart into the space around you, into the trees, plants, grass, earth, and other living beings. As you do so, hold the intention in your heart: *I offer my love to you.* As you breathe in, visualize the breath of the trees, plants, grass, and other living beings flowing into your heart as an energy.

Continue this for 10 minutes,
or longer if you'd like.

When you feel ready, take a moment before you get up and go about your day.

Perhaps over time what you breathe in may make its presence known as a response, one that can be felt and even heard.

FOURTEEN

Step

In beauty I walk,

With beauty before me, I walk

With beauty behind me, I walk

With beauty above me, I walk

With beauty all around me, I walk

With beauty within me, I walk

In beauty it is finished

—TRADITIONAL DINÉ PRAYER[17]

We are a walking species. For most of human history, we moved solely on foot, placing one step after another. This form of movement is as old as we are, as present in the depths of our being as our relationship with the living Earth. When we migrated out of Africa over sixty thousand years ago, reaching all corners of the world, we walked. The journalist Paul Salopek has spent over a decade retracing this ancient route, walking at the speed of three miles an hour, from the Horn of Africa all the way to Tierra del Fuego at the tip of South America. In a conversation I had with him, he reflected on the sense of timelessness that walking creates and the ways it can instill a sense of peace.

> I think that this sense of well-being that comes with timelessness, the sense of being at peace—it must be very, very old. And it must be like a stylus dropping into a groove on the surface of a planet and making this music. And we are, our bodies are, that stylus, and we're meant to move at this RPM that comes with the movement of our body.[18]

Throughout the ages many cultures have held a deep understanding of the importance of walking, not just as a means of migration or reaching our destination, but as a vehicle of transformation. Pilgrims, from Japan's Shikoku Pilgrimage to Spain's Camino de Santiago, journeyed along the pilgrimage path in a space of reflection and prayer, often experiencing a profound sense of embodied devotion with each step. In recent years, long trails like the 2,650-mile Pacific Crest Trail and 2,190-mile Appalachian Trail have become increasingly popular among hikers who are often seeking this sense of timelessness and peace that arises from a long, slow journey on foot away from the relentless pace of modern life.

But one doesn't need to walk across the world, embark on a pilgrimage, or hike thousands of miles on a trail to tune in to the ancient rhythm that aligns our bodies with the movement of the Earth. What naturally begins to unfold on extended walking pilgrimages—the slowing of the mind, the calming of the body, a deepening connection to the landscapes around us—can be achieved through intentional walking as we place one foot in front of the other and walk upon Her body. When we join the awareness of breath and the feeling of love in the heart with the ancient rhythm of walking, we are able to step into the present moment—a space of devotion—and into the arms of the Earth as She stretches out before us.

So often when we walk, we do so without intention, consumed by our worries, emotions, and thoughts. It's as if we are moving in a bubble of our own projected self-image, unaware of the ground beneath our feet or what is unfolding around us in the present moment. Phones and earbuds have only made this disconnection more acute as we gaze down at our screens, our ears closed to the outside world. Yet it doesn't take much to break this spell. When we engage the ancient cycles of breath, heart, and step, the simple act of walking becomes a profound practice of awareness, devotion, and ultimately, communion.

I have long walked in alignment with my breath and the presence of love in my heart, practicing a walking dhikr, remembering the Beloved with each step. Over the last decade, I have integrated a direct prayer for the Earth into my practice of walking in remembrance of God and have found it to be a remarkably potent way to enter more deeply into a space of devotion and kinship with Her. The practices described below are all ones I have done daily for many years along the trails near my home, the shoreline of the Pacific, or the city streets of London.

The remarkable thing about these practices is not only their simplicity, but that you can do them *anywhere* you walk. And while it is, of course, nice to do them in a landscape devoid of human development and the noise of our modern world, they can be just as potent while walking in the midst of life with all its mess and contradictions. When I walk in a city, I like to think of it as a little act of rebellion, bringing the remembrance of the sacred nature of creation through my steps as I walk atop the pavement. For as much as we have tried to cover Her, layering Her with asphalt and concrete, and our forgetfulness, She is always there, just beneath our feet.

The following three step practices build on each other, incorporating new elements as they unfold. I suggest moving through them sequentially to start, until you are familiar with them.

I

ALIGNING BREATH AND STEP

Approx. 45 minutes

Find a location where you can walk for a good distance in a setting where the living world feels close and tangible. In an urban space this could be a park or along a riverside or canal path. If you are near a wilder landscape, this could be on a trail through a meadow, forest, or wetland.

Before you begin your walk, find somewhere to sit.

Close your eyes and focus on the breath. On the out-breath, visualize or sense energy flowing from the space at the top of the inhale down into the heart. On the in-breath, visualize or sense energy rising up through the chest and neck and then flowing out through the top of the head.

As you continue breathing and visualizing this cycle, you will begin to feel a subtle energetic expansion in the heart as it becomes infused by the energy of the breath. Place your conscious awareness on this feeling of expansion in the heart.

Continue for 5–10 minutes.

Open your eyes, stand up, and begin walking at a steady, comfortable pace. Over the first couple of minutes, adjust your pace to match the rhythm of your breath, settling into a simple moving meditation. (I find that taking two or three steps per in-breath and two or three steps per out-breath creates a natural, steady rhythm for me. Find your own pace.)

As you walk, thoughts will naturally arise, or you will be distracted by something around you. When this happens, return your attention to the cycle of your breath and the rhythm of your step. Out-breath: one, two, three; in-breath: one, two, three.

Continue for 30 minutes,
or longer if you'd like.

II

WALKING AND BREATHING
WITH THE EARTH

Approx. 45 minutes

Find a location where you can walk for a good distance in a setting where the living world feels close and tangible.

Before you begin your walk, find somewhere to sit.

Close your eyes and focus on the breath. On the out-breath, visualize or sense energy flowing from the space at the top of the inhale down into the heart. On the in-breath, visualize or sense energy rising up through the chest and neck and then flowing out through the top of the head.

As you continue breathing and visualizing this cycle, you will begin to feel a subtle energetic expansion in the heart as it becomes infused by the energy of the breath. Place your conscious awareness on this feeling of expansion in the heart.

Continue for 5–10 minutes.

Open your eyes, stand up, and begin your walk, adjusting your pace to match the rhythm of your breath, settling into a simple moving meditation. (I find that taking two or three steps per in-breath and two or three steps per out-breath creates a natural, steady rhythm for me. Find your own pace.)

After a few minutes of walking, begin to visualize your out-breath as energy flowing down through your body and into the Earth beneath your feet. And on the in-breath, visualize the breath as energy rising up out of the Earth and through your body to the top of your head.

As thoughts arise, return your awareness to the cycle of breath moving between you and the Earth.

As you deepen into this space of breathing in relationship with the Earth as you walk, notice how it makes you feel. Does your body feel more grounded? Do you feel more present? Do you feel Her beneath your feet?

Continue for 30 minutes,
or longer if you'd like.

III

WALKING IN REMEMBRANCE

Approx. 45 minutes

Find a location where you can walk for a good distance in a setting where the living world feels close and tangible.

Before you begin your walk find somewhere to sit.

Close your eyes and focus on the breath. On the out-breath, visualize or sense energy flowing from the space at the top of the inhale down into the heart. On the in-breath, visualize or sense energy rising up through the chest and neck and then flowing out through the top of the head.

As you continue breathing and visualizing this cycle, you will begin to feel a subtle energetic expansion in the heart as it becomes infused by the energy of the breath. Place your conscious awareness on this feeling of expansion in the heart.

Continue for 5–10 minutes.

Open your eyes, stand up, and begin your walk, adjusting your pace to match the rhythm of your breath, settling into a simple moving meditation. (I find that taking two or three steps per in-breath and two or three steps per out-breath creates a natural, steady rhythm for me. Find your own pace.)

After a few minutes of walking, begin to visualize your out-breath as energy flowing down through your body and into the Earth beneath your feet. And on the in-breath, visualize the breath as energy rising up out of the Earth and through your body to the top of your head.

After a few minutes of walking and settling into this cycle of breathing with the Earth, focus your attention on your heart, and on the out-breath silently say: *I remember you.*

Continue for some time.

As you repeat this silent mantra of remembrance as you walk, allow yourself to deepen into the space of gratitude you feel for the Earth and all She provides you. Hold this awareness in your heart.

Now add another line to the mantra, but this time on your in-breath silently say: *I am so grateful for all you offer* as you breathe in from the Earth beneath your feet, adding another layer to the cycle. On the out-breath silently say *I remember you*, and on the in-breath, *I am so grateful for all you offer.*

Continue with this mantra as you walk.

While it is helpful when learning these practices to walk in an environment where the living world feels close, I encourage you to also do them in the city or an urban space and to not let the setting dictate whether or not you walk in remembrance. In the end this can be a practice of devotion you do everywhere you walk, so you are in remembrance not only on the trail or in a park but also on the way to work, to school, in the grocery store, and all the places in-between, for She is present everywhere.

Listening

Do you remember how you came into existence?
You may not remember
because you arrived a little drunk.
Let me give you a hint:
Let go of your mind and then be mindful.
Close your ears and listen!
—RŪMĪ[19]

I rise early, before dawn, to pray. In the spring I open my window wide to hear the chorus of birdsong filling the landscape around my home, the sound combining with the clicking of my prayer beads as they move slowly through my fingers. As spring moves toward summer, the arrival of the Swainson's thrush brings a spiraling polyphonic melody that pervades the air, its distinct call emanating toward me as an invitation. Then, come fall, the rains return, and with them a many-layered hush settles over the grateful and thirsty forest. In my meditation I dance between absence and presence as the rain, wind, birds, and the many other songs of the Earth reveal themselves in a continuous, unfolding expression of Her multiplicity.

As much as we are a walking species, we are a listening one, and from the beginning of our human story we have been immersed in the constant presence of Her symphony. The Earth is awash in sound, and has been since Her beginning. As She evolved, the richness of Her sonic expressions grew into a many-voiced chorus, one that reveals the oneness within life's remarkable diversity. The songs of birds, the drumming of rain, the whispering and howling of winds are just a few of the many voices She shares with us. These sounds and songs were woven into the primal fabric of our being, affirming the sacred substance of sound as a manifestation of the wondrous nature of creation.

In our modern era of forgetfulness we have added layers of sound to the Earth, many of which are drowning out Her voices and Her song. The constant thrum of machines—cars, planes, construction equipment, air conditioners, leaf blowers—fills the air, not just as noise but as a veil of separation, drawing us further from Her and making it harder not only to hear Her but to truly listen. As these veils accumulate, we grow more and more distant from Her, and it becomes increasingly challenging to recognize and acknowledge Her presence. For real listening is an acknowledgment, a recognition not only of sound, song, and voice, but of the beings who offer them.

As we seek to embody a spiritual ecology, listening must become a central aspect of awakening the memory of our primordial covenant of relationship with the living Earth. When we listen, we uncover those ancient ties of kinship that were woven into us through song and sound over millennia. And as much as we have covered the Earth in the noise of modern life, She is still there always singing beneath the din of our human world. If we place our attention there, we may find it is not so difficult to break through those layers to recognize the voices of the more-than-human, to hear Her voice, and to begin listening again.

Relearning to listen must involve the heart, this conduit of love that serves as a bridge between the outer and inner senses. In Sufism we speak of the inner senses as the eyes and ears of the heart. When the ears of the heart become activated, it allows us not only to listen more deeply but to absorb the presence of the voices we hear and the ones who offer them. It helps open us to the kinship we share with the living world, reweaving our relationship with Her as we listen. It can even allow the origin of that voice to penetrate us.

Through this something else quite remarkable can happen. Over time (and it does take time), the Earth may begin to take notice that we are listening. And when She does, She may choose to speak—not necessarily through words, or in a language we understand (though She can if She wants to), or in forms we might expect, but rather as a *presence*, one that can make itself known in waking consciousness, prayer, meditation, and even in our dreams. Like the Earth Herself, it's all deeply mysterious.

The following three practices are rooted in listening from the heart, building on the preceding heart practices (see pages 163–69). Over the years I have spent countless hours with them, walking and sitting by the shore listening to the breaking waves, standing among the trees as the winds move through their branches and leaves, and being immersed in the dawn chorus as I pray and meditate.

I have found that in that space of love we can learn to experience the waters and the wind anew, to hear many voices both as individuals and as One, and to listen to the silence that exists between absence and presence, for that silence is also very much a sound.

The following three listening practices build on each other, incorporating new elements as they unfold. I suggest moving through them sequentially to start, until you are familiar with them.

I

WATER

Approx. 45 minutes

Locate a moving body of water near where you live. This could be the ocean, a bay, a waterfall, a river, or a creek or stream—somewhere water makes a sound as it breaks upon the shore or babbles as it flows.

If you're able to walk there, begin with the walking and breathing with the Earth practice (see page 176) to bring you into your heart and a space of connection with the Earth. If you need to drive or use public transportation, do the breathing with the heart practice (see page 163) for ten to fifteen minutes once you arrive. This will help ground you in the space within the heart that you need to listen from. If needed, spend more time with either of these practices until you feel fully present in your heart.

Find somewhere comfortable to sit or lie where you can clearly hear the sounds of the waves or the movement of the water. Choose a place where you'll be able to relax and focus your full attention on listening. If you are by the ocean, make sure you face the ocean and sit or lie at a safe distance to allow for the changing tide.

Close your eyes and focus your attention on the single voice of the breaking waves or the moving water of the river or stream. Try to block out all the other sounds you hear around you—people, cars, birds, etc.—so that your awareness rests on the sound of the water. Let this sound wash over you.

Continue for a few minutes.

Awash in the general sound of the waves or flowing water, identify the distinct sounds present within it. Notice how the sounds of breaking waves vary depending on the size of the shore break, and hear the swoosh of the water as each wave recedes. Listen to the way the water babbles and gurgles and ripples as it flows downstream and breaks over rocks. Locate the different timbres within the layers of the river or stream or each breaking wave. Place your attention on each of these subtle variations for a few moments. Consider how together they make up the voice of the waves or river, just like different sustained notes form a chord on a piano.

Continue for a few minutes.

As you breathe, visualize your in-breath as the voice of the waves, river, or stream entering your ears, moving through your body, and settling into your heart.

Continue for 10 minutes.

As you continue visualizing the voice of the water entering your ears, body, and heart on the in-breath, hold the intention: *I hear you.*

Continue for 5 minutes.

After this acknowledgment, spend a few minutes holding the intention in your heart: *I offer my love to you.*

When you feel ready, open your eyes and take a moment before you get up and go about your day.

This practice of listening can be applied to any voice or sound. You can do it with any more-than-human voice that expresses itself in a constant offering of sound: rain, croaking frogs, chirping crickets, and more. You can do this with birds, of course, and the third practice of this chapter is specific to birdsong (see page 191).

II

WIND

Approx. 45 minutes

Choose a day with some wind, ideally enough so you can hear its distinct voice as it rustles the branches and leaves of nearby trees or even gives a little howl now and then. Avoid days when the wind is gusty or stormy and it becomes less agreeable to be outside and harder to focus.

Locate a forest, woodland, or park with trees near where you live. There should be enough trees for you to clearly hear the movement of wind through the branches and leaves and a variety of sounds.

If you're able to walk there, begin with the walking and breathing with the Earth practice (see page 176) to bring you into your heart and a space of connection with the Earth. If you need to drive or use public transport, do the breathing with the heart practice (see page 163) for ten to fifteen minutes once you arrive. This will help ground you in the space within the heart from which to listen. If needed, spend more time with this practice until you feel fully present in your heart.

Find a comfortable place to sit or lie down by the trees where you can hear the wind as it blows through the branches and leaves. Choose a place where you'll be relaxed and able to focus your full attention on listening.

Close your eyes and focus on the voice of the wind as it moves through the trees. Let this sound wash over you.

Continue for a few minutes.

Awash in the general voice of the wind as it moves through the trees, begin to identify the distinct sounds present within it—the varying degrees of whispers, murmurs, hums, and howls of the wind. Listen for the sounds of the branches swaying and creaking, the leaves rustling and whooshing. Notice how the sounds shift depending on the type of tree the wind blows through, and notice how the size and shape of the leaves create subtle variations in the wind's vocalizations. Place your attention on each of these different offerings of the wind.

Continue for a few minutes.

As you listen deeply to these different expressions of sound, ask yourself: *Which is wind, and which is branch or leaf? Where does the wind end and the branches and leaves begin? Is it in conversation with the trees that the wind makes its voice known? Where does one voice become many?*

Reflect on these questions for a few minutes.

As you absorb this conversation taking place all around you, return to your breath. Visualize your in-breath as the voices of the wind, branches, and leaves entering through your ears, moving through your body, and settling into your heart.

Continue for 10 minutes.

Continue visualizing this unfolding exchange of voices entering your ears, body, and heart. As you do so, hold the intention: *I hear you.*

Continue for 5 minutes.

After this acknowledgment, spend a few minutes holding the intention in your heart: *I offer my love to you.*

When you feel ready, open your eyes and take a moment before you get up and go about your day.

This practice isn't limited to the wind but can be done in any landscape where the voices of the more-than-human are in conversation: forests, meadows, wetlands, parks, gardens, and beyond. You can also pay attention to the relationship between the more-than-human and human voices and sounds and the conversation unfolding there, even if it feels mostly one-sided.

III

THE DAWN CHORUS

Approx. 1 hour

The dawn chorus, that remarkable outpouring of birdsong that begins before the light of day, is mostly a seasonal affair. Unless you live in the tropics, it is in the spring months that you can experience this wonder of sound and song. Where I live in Northern California, this chorus usually begins in late March and peaks in mid- to late May. In addition to being a powerful listening experience, I find that being immersed in the dawn chorus is a wonderful way to participate in spring's expressions of revelation as the season turns toward summer. For me, there is no greater way to begin one's day, or to celebrate this season, than in prayer and meditation, awash in this chorus of voices. I recommend doing this practice often during spring.

If you don't already know of a place near your home where the dawn chorus is abundant, do some research and locate an ideal listening location to do this practice.

Arise early before the dawn chorus starts, which is usually thirty minutes to an hour before sunrise. Plan to arrive at your listening location just before the dawn chorus begins. Dress warmly so you are comfortable. Consider bringing a flask of hot tea with you and something to sit or lie on that will keep you dry.

When you arrive at your listening location, find somewhere to sit or lie down where you will be comfortable for the next hour.

Close your eyes and begin doing the breathing with the heart practice (see page 163): On the out-breath, visualize or sense energy flowing from the space at the top of the inhale down into the heart. On the in-breath, visualize or sense energy rising up through the chest and neck and then flowing out through the top of the head. Feel the subtle energetic expansion in the heart as it becomes infused by the energy of the breath. Continue breathing with the heart throughout this practice.

As each bird offers its voice to the landscape, let the sound wash over you, acknowledging it with the awareness of your attention. Notice the different bird voices that slowly reveal themselves as the darkness turns to twilight. Pay attention to how distinct each offering of birdsong is and how every song is a gesture of the bird's presence.

Pay attention to the space and silence between the offerings of birdsong and how the forest or landscape receives their presence. Notice how the absence of sound becomes an echo to the call of birdsong.

As dawn approaches and more and more birdsong fills the air, listen to the call-and-response, the interplay and overlap, as individual voices become a chorus. Let this offering of sound and song envelop you like a warm blanket, covering you in its beauty. Sink into this space, a space of absence and presence, of voice and chorus.

Now put your attention more directly on your heart. Visualize immersing these voices of birds, this chorus, this wall of sound, into your heart. Drown the sound in the space of love that is present there. Merge into this space of love and song, or absence and presence.

Continue this until after the sun has risen.

Open your eyes, adjust to the morning light, sit, and have some hot tea. The day is beginning.

SIXTEEN

Time

A lie is a truth removed from its time-place.
—TYSON YUNKAPORTA[20]

If you walk the same trail most days of the year, you begin to notice things. The turning of the seasons reveals itself in slow increments of nuanced expression: mushrooms emerging after the first good rains, debris from fallen branches after a big winter storm, acacia blossoms bursting open in the height of spring, and the sounds of crickets in the tall summer grass. Walk that trail for years and you come to know a place intimately. You witness earth, blackened and scorched by fire, become a forest, seeded by the cones of the bishop pine. Trees at first huddled together so thick you can't walk through them begin to thin out as the competition for sunlight leads to growth for some and eventual death for others. You notice how time expresses itself in relation to place. And a kinship forms.

Time unfolds in cycles: day into night within the Earth's twenty-four-hour rotation, the changing seasons within our yearly circumambulation around the sun. Within these cycles lie countless others: the lunar cycle, the rise and fall of the tides, the migration patterns of birds and butterflies, the fleeting expression of a flower blossom, and, within it all, the ever-present movement of our shared breath. Everything in creation has its own cycle, its own expression of time, each one existing in relationship with every other, like interlocking circles inside an endless series of nesting dolls. It's a vast, mysterious, and wondrous manifestation of the ways love flows through all things.

Yet despite this fundamental truth, and its centrality to all that exists, we have linearized time into something so straight it's barely recognizable. It's not just that we have digitized or atomized time, but that we have stripped it of rhythm and place, flattened it—and named that "progress." It's almost as if time now hovers, disconnected from the Earth, suspended in a vacuum far removed from its most physical and tangible forms. And perhaps most dangerously of all, we have attempted to remove time from its relationship to land.

The cycle of a day is experienced differently everywhere on Earth. The expression of the seasons not only differs dramatically between the Northern and Southern Hemispheres and the equator, but can be completely distinct within just a hundred miles—with different trees, plants, flowers, birds, and topographies (here the list is truly endless) all manifesting a different expression of light and season within their own cycle of time. The sound of a dawn chorus is unique all over the world, not just because each chorus is made up of different species of birds, but also because each location is unique.

Each place has its own time, and within that time many layers exist. That place is a landscape, and a forest within that landscape, and a tree within that forest, and so on. Each form of creation is an expression of place as much as it is an expression of time. The bishop pine that grew out of serotiny, seeded into scorched earth, is not the same as the bishop pine a hundred miles away. Encoded in that tree is the memory of fire that was its birth and the land it grows from. It carries that imprint in its yearly layering of wood, marking our circumambulation around the sun. Its unique expression as a being is a reflection of the place that is its home as much as the species it belongs to. When we flatten time and remove it from place, that unique being becomes just a bishop pine, a species, and finally just a tree, uprooted from the ground that moors it, floating in abstraction. And love, too, begins to recede.

When we recognize each form of creation as its own cycle of time and as an expression of place, something begins to shift. The lie is laid bare, we again begin to see the truth of the cycles around us, and a space of kinship beckons. And just like when we listen, it is our intention and attention that support this shift, allowing us to recognize each unique being as a cycle of time and its own expression of place. Once we begin to do this, and especially when it is done repeatedly over time—walking the same trail over the course of a year, experiencing the rhythm of the seasons come and go, spending a half hour with a tree and returning each week or each month—we become more connected to place. Our cycles attune to the cycles around us, free from the veil of separation that abstract, flattened time imposes. We become more rooted, and our ability to be attentive, and more in tune with seasons, deepens.

These practices—walking with the awareness of cycles rooted in place, walking the same path over a cycle of the seasons, and visiting the same tree regularly—can reveal a deepening understanding of, and relationship with, time and place. Like the preceding practices, they draw on the simple spiritual technologies of the breath and the heart to cultivate presence and activate love. For love is what lies at the center of time, as it is the axis of all things.

The following three time practices build on each other, incorporating new elements as they unfold. I suggest moving through them sequentially to start, until you are familiar with them.

I

OBSERVING CYCLES IN A LANDSCAPE

Approx. 1 hour

Find a trail or a park not too far from your home—ideally one with a variety of trees and plants. Choose a place where you can walk comfortably for about an hour.

Begin your walk and adjust your pace to match the rhythm of your breath, settling into a simple moving meditation.

After a few minutes of walking, begin to visualize your out-breath as energy flowing down through your body and into the Earth beneath your feet. And on the in-breath, visualize the breath as energy rising up out of the Earth and through your body to the top of your head.

Be conscious of the cyclical nature of this practice: the cycle of your in- and out-breath, the visualization of that breath flowing in a loop into the Earth beneath your feet and up through your body, the cycle of your steps moving in relation to the breath. Notice the rhythm within you unfolding as you walk.

Continue for a few minutes.

As you walk, be attentive to all the more-than-human beings you encounter: the trees, the bushes, the flowers, the birds, the insects buzzing around you. As you see or hear them, consider how each being exists within its own rhythm, its own cycle of time.

After a while stop in front of a rooted more-than-human being: a tree, or bush, or flower. Consider its cycle of time and how it is connected to the earth it grows from. Reflect on how the earth is a connective tissue between this being and the other rooted beings nearby, how it connects to all the rooted expressions of time you see.

Continue walking and stopping in front of different rooted beings. Notice how each being you encounter, even if it is the same species you have already encountered, is unique. Notice whether it is taller or shorter, how it sits in relation to the landscape, and how it sits in relation to the sun. Ask yourself how the place in which this being is rooted is reflected in its uniqueness.

Bring your awareness to the fact that you are not a physically rooted being. Your feet do not grow roots that moor you to the earth and the landscape. Then consider how your awareness of the more-than-human beings rooted in place can act like a root; how the awareness of their unique cycles of time, and their unique relation to place, allows you to acknowledge them more deeply; and how this acknowledgment is a connection, the beginnings of kinship that can help you become rooted to them, and through them to place.

*Continue walking, observing
cycles, growing roots.*

II

A YEARLONG WALK

Approx. 1 hour (each time you do it)

Find a trail or a park not too far from your home—ideally one with a variety of trees and plants—that you can return to regularly over the period of a year. Choose a place you can walk comfortably for about an hour.

Begin your walk and adjust your pace to match the rhythm of your breath, settling into a simple moving meditation.

After a few minutes of walking, begin to visualize your out-breath as energy flowing down through your body and into the Earth beneath your feet. And on the in-breath, visualize the breath as energy rising up out of the Earth and through your body to the top of your head.

Be conscious of the cyclical nature of this practice: the cycle of your in- and out-breath, the visualization of that breath flowing in a cycle into the Earth beneath your feet and up through your body, the cycle of your steps moving in relation to the breath. Notice the rhythm, the cycles within you unfolding as you walk.

*Do this practice each time
you take this walk.*

As you walk, be attentive to all the more-than-human beings you encounter: the trees, the bushes, the flowers, the birds, the insects buzzing around you. As you see or hear them, consider how each being exists within its own rhythm, within its own cycle of time. Consider how they embody the season. Are the budding trees, the presence of blossoms, and the vibrancy of color expressing an aspect of spring? Whatever the season is when you begin your yearlong walk, take note, for it marks the beginning of a full cycle of engagement.

Continue your walk in
this state of awareness.

Next time you take this walk, take note of what has changed and what has remained the same. How is the season expressing itself this time as you walk?

Ask yourself this question
each time you walk.

By the third or fourth walk, certain rooted beings may begin to stand out to you, to call to you. Stop in front of them and acknowledge them. Notice how this being sits in relation to the landscape, how it expresses the season at this particular moment. Ask yourself how the place in which this being is rooted is reflected in its uniqueness.

As the weeks go by and turn into months, reflect on how your relationship with the more-than-human beings you encounter has shifted. Do you feel an intimacy with them, especially with the rooted beings you have stopped beside regularly?

As you witness the seasons turn, ask yourself: *How does this place tell time? What makes it unique?*

As more weeks go by, reflect on the connection you feel with your rooted friends, with this place. Do you feel a kinship, a sense of love even?

After a year passes, consider continuing to walk, to keep noticing, to keep expanding your cycle of time

III

KINSHIP TIME

Approx. 30 minutes

Before beginning this practice refamiliarize yourself with the shared breath practice (page 156), as steps within that practice are also used here.

Find a large rooted being near where you live that intrigues you or calls to you and that you would like to spend time with on a regular basis. It can live along the path of your yearlong walk practice, or somewhere else—it doesn't matter, as long as it's easy for you to get to and from your home.

As you walk to visit this being, adjust your pace to match the rhythm of your breath, settling into a simple moving meditation.

After a few minutes of walking, begin to visualize your out-breath as energy flowing down through your body and into the Earth beneath your feet. And on the in-breath, visualize the breath as energy rising up out of the Earth and through your body to the top of your head.

When you arrive, stand before the rooted being and take it in. Spend a few minutes noticing its height, width, branches, leaves, colors, the texture of its bark. See how it's rooted in place. Are the roots spread out, visible, buckling just below the surface, or are they mostly hidden? Notice how this being sits in relation to the landscape, how it expresses the season at this particular moment. Ask yourself how the place in which this being is rooted is reflected in its uniqueness. How old do you think it is?

Acknowledge it with a simple "hello," or another greeting that feels right to you. This can be audible or silent.

Find somewhere to sit in front of this being where you will be comfortable for the next half hour. As you sit before it, visualize your out-breath as an offering of energy from your essence into the rooted being.

Focus on this for a few minutes.

Now hold the awareness that what you are breathing out is carbon dioxide. Visualize it dispersing into the air and being absorbed by the rooted being in front of you. On your in-breath, hold in your awareness that you are breathing in oxygen offered by this same being.

Focus on this cycle for a few minutes.

Reflect on how your cycle of breath is functioning in relation to its breath: how you breathe at a different pace, averaging fifteen breaths a minute, while this rooted being is in a continuous cycle of respiration that expresses itself differently than yours. And how, though you don't breathe like a rooted being and it doesn't breathe like you, there is a shared breath, a meeting of cycles.

Now let go of your focus on the exchange of carbon dioxide and oxygen. Instead, visualize your out-breath as energy entering the being in front of you and being absorbed by it. As you breathe in, visualize the breath offered by this being entering your body as a life force, a gift that nourishes you.

Focus on this cycle for a few minutes.

In this space of exchange, consider how the coming together of your cycle and its cycle allows you to step into a greater cycle of time, one that is larger than each on its own. It isn't about how old you are, or how old it is, or how many breaths each of you takes. Rather, it is a shared experience of time manifesting in a space of mutual exchange—all unfolding in the specific place this rooted being exists within. It is both rooted and rootless, timeless and timebound.

Before you leave, offer your gratitude to this being. It can be as simple as "thank you," offered audibly or silently.

When you next visit, repeat this practice but start by noticing what's changed. Is there new growth? Does the change in the way the light hits this being shift the way you see it in relation to this place it's rooted in? How are the season's movements being reflected by this being?

Visit as frequently as you can and watch what happens, both with your outer senses and your inner ones. Does love begin to grow? Does kinship blossom? Ask yourself: *Is that experience also a cycle of time? Is it rooted in this place?*

SEVENTEEN

Prayer

If the heart is praying it is all right! If your heart has
heard your prayer, God has heard it!
—PERSIAN SUFI SONG[21]

Over the years I would often hear my father share a couplet
from a Persian Sufi song when speaking about prayer. They
were lines his teacher's teacher, the great Indian Sufi saint
Radha Mohan Lal, used to recite and sing: "If the heart is
praying it is alright! If your heart has heard your prayer, God
has heard it!" I heard these words so many times it was as if
they were impressed into me, almost as if they were a prayer.

When I was growing up, my father never really gave
me specific prayers to memorize, aside from the dhikr, the
constant recollection of the name of God practiced with
the breath. Instead he taught me *how* to pray. It wasn't that
he thought words and specific prayers didn't have power
and potency, which of course they do, but that one should

place one's primary focus in one's heart. The heart is where a prayer should be offered from, for it is the principal conduit between you and the Divine, a space of awareness where love is present and where the veils of separation between you and the Divine can be lessened, allowing your prayers to be more directly offered and more fully received.

My father did, of course, have many prayers that he loved and practiced, which he would reference in his writings and teachings. But alongside this, he would almost always speak about the individual nature of prayer and how it is a reflection of the unique relationship that each soul has with God. He often recited the well-known saying, "There are as many ways to God as there are human beings," and perhaps the lesser known, "If you leave a human being alone, they will find their own way back to God." To me these spoke not only of the numerous religions and traditions and individual ways through which we can encounter the Divine, but also of prayer itself—how through prayer we find our own way of speaking with the Divine, in all Their forms, and how it is in the end a rather intimate conversation between us and Them. Over time prayer reveals the unique note of offering we hold within our heart, the love it contains, and how this is ultimately a space of communion.

Throughout my life I've offered many different prayers at different times: prayers asking for forgiveness and prayers offering thanks; prayers uttered by others that seek to draw one closer to the Divine, like Ibn 'Arabi's "Oh Lord, nourish me not with love but the desire for love";[22] and increasingly, prayers of my own making that are often very simple in nature, just a few words that feel as much gesture as phrase. As my relationship with the Earth has deepened, I have also included Her more and more directly in my prayers: asking Her for forgiveness when I feel Her cry, offering my gratitude when I receive Her grace and bounty, and offering my love and awe for Her ceaseless giving. And under all this, woven between the prayers in the space between the notes, is my desire to be in constant remembrance of Her, so that an offering is made to Her on each out-breath, and in return I am immersed in Her on each in-breath, so She is alive and present with each footstep, with each glance, with each sound and song. So that there is no moment She is not within my heart, no moment when I am not offering my remembrance to Her.

The preceding practices of breath, heart, step, listening, and time are, to me, all prayers that can help open our hearts to awareness and remembrance of Her. They are easily integrated into everyday life and designed to be done often, to help bring praise for the Earth into our most basic actions. You can weave prayer directly into these practices however you feel called, with words or with silence. Additionally, there will always be special moments or occasions when you feel called to celebrate Her: when basking in Her

abundance or to ask for forgiveness for your own forgetfulness or for the pain that others' forgetfulness causes Her.
You will be called to praise Her as you are greeted by the
dawn chorus or witness the mist hanging over a meadow
before it's burned off by the sun or sit before a rooted
being—and in all the ways Her beauty overcomes you.
There is no wrong way to pray, no limit to prayer, no voice
that She doesn't want to hear. What words you offer, if any,
are up to you, as it is you She wants to hear from—it is your
unique offering of remembrance She asks for.

But whatever you say, whatever you do, I invite you to
offer it from the heart.

I

SOME WORDS

For me, prayer, whether an offering of words or of silence, always begins by putting my attention on my heart and evoking love there. Before you offer prayers, start by spending a moment with the breathing with the heart practice to bring you into a space of awareness and love within the heart.

Close your eyes and focus on the breath. On the out-breath, visualize or sense energy flowing from the space at the top of the inhale down into the heart. On the in-breath, visualize or sense energy rising up through the chest and neck and then flowing out through the top of the head.

As you continue breathing and visualizing this cycle, you will begin to feel a subtle energetic expansion in the heart as it becomes infused by the energy of the breath. Place your conscious awareness on this feeling of expansion in the heart.

The following words are a few simple examples of prayers you might offer and are meant to serve as a starting point if you need one. Prayer is a gateway into the vastness of the heart and what lies beyond it: a place that no words can ever encompass. Rather, these words can serve as an invitation and offering, the beginning of a conversation with the Divine in all Their forms.

A prayer for breathing: *Beloved Mother, I offer my remembrance to You with this breath.*

A prayer for walking: *Beloved Mother, let my steps walk upon the Earth in remembrance of You.*

A prayer for listening: *Beloved Mother, I offer my ears to You and Your songs.*

A prayer for acknowledging Her: *Beloved Mother, I see You, I hear You, I feel Your presence, and I offer You mine.*

A prayer for witnessing Her suffering: *Beloved Mother, I hear Your cry, I hear Your suffering.*

A prayer to ask for forgiveness: *Beloved Mother, forgive us for what we have done to You. Forgive us for our forgetfulness.*

A prayer for Her beauty: *Beloved Mother, thank You for this gift of beauty, for its grace.*

A prayer for thanks: *Beloved Mother, thank You for all that You give, for all that You offer us.*

II

YOUR WORDS

Formulate your own prayers to offer to the Earth. They can be based on the previous practice's words or be completely different. They can be for these actions and feelings, or for any way you engage with the Earth and feel called to pray and offer your remembrance to Her. They can be a few words or many. It doesn't matter. What matters is that they feel genuine to you and you offer them from the heart.

Close your eyes and focus on the breath. On the out-breath, visualize or sense energy flowing from the space at the top of the inhale down into the heart. On the in-breath, visualize or sense energy rising up through the chest and neck and then flowing out through the top of the head.

As you continue breathing and visualizing this cycle, you will begin to feel a subtle energetic expansion in the heart as it becomes infused by the energy of the breath. Place your conscious awareness on this feeling of expansion in the heart.

Continue for a few minutes.

Begin your own prayer: *Beloved Mother . . .*

III

NO WORDS

Silence is its own form of prayer, a unique offering of its own, a space to receive and envelop the Earth in your heart. Ultimately, it is a space of sustained presence, one that can exist between the notes of our spoken or silent utterances. Like the words we use to speak, silence is a language, a form of expression that belongs to the heart. It is as unique as our fingerprints. In this space, the heart takes over, weaving threads of love and remembrance of the sacred nature of creation, of the Beloved, of the great love affair that exists between us. For me, silence, like love, is at the heart of everything.

Here is but one simple beginning, a simple silent prayer of thanks. The rest I leave to you.

Hold the awareness in your heart of all that She offers us.

On your out-breath, visualize the love in your heart being offered as remembrance to the Earth. Spend a moment or two breathing out this love as a silent prayer.

Then on your in-breath, visualize placing the Earth inside your heart. Spend a moment or two breathing in this love as a silent prayer.

Here, in silence, a conversation begins . . .

ACKNOWLEDGMENTS

To my father, for your teachings, love, and presence. To Jenn Brown at Shambhala, for the initial invitation to write this book and your support throughout the process. To Seana Quinn, for helping me see how to adapt a series of lectures into something more. To Michelle Moore, for your keen copyedits and clarity. To the team at *Emergence Magazine*, for your brilliant work and the spirit of service you embody. And to Cleary, for the love and grace you offer each day.

NOTES

1. "'The Great Unraveling': an ongoing collapse of living structures. This is what happens when ecological, biological, and social systems are commodified through an industrial growth society or 'business as usual' frame." Joanna Macy, "Entering the Bardo," *Emergence Magazine*, July 20, 2020, https://emergencemagazine.org/op_ed/entering-the-bardo/.

2. Thomas Berry first introduced the idea of "the great conversation" in *The Dream of the Earth* (Sierra Club Books, 1988), 18. He later expanded on this theme in *Befriending the Earth: A Theology of Reconciliation Between Humans and the Earth*, coauthored with Thomas Clarke (Twenty-Third Publications, 1991).

3. N. Scott Momaday, *Earth Keeper: Reflections on the American Land* (Harper, 2020), 12.

4. Natalie Diaz, "The Water Is the First Body," in *Postcolonial Love Poem* (Graywolf Press, 2020), 46.

5. A *hadith qudsi* is a saying attributed to God through the Prophet Muhammad (peace be upon him). The hadith qudsi "I was a Hidden Treasure and I loved to be known, so I created the world that I might be known" does not appear in the canonical collections of

hadith such as Sahih Bukhari or Sahih Muslim and is not formally recognized by hadith scholars. This hadith is primarily associated with Sufi interpretations of Islam, particularly the teachings of Ibn 'Arabi, who used it to express the concept of *wahdat al-wujūd* (Oneness of Being) in which creation is understood as a divine act of love and self-disclosure.

6. Thomas Berry, "What Does the Earth Desire?" interview, The Gaia Foundation Summit, May 2003, https://thomasberry.org/thomas-berry-what-does-the-earth-desire.

7. Paraphrased from Bertolt Brecht's poem "Motto": "In the dark times, will there also be singing? / Yes, there will be singing. / About the dark times." Bertolt Brecht, *Poems 1913–1956*, trans. John Willett (Routledge, Chapman and Hall, 1976), 660.

8. Quoted in Llewellyn Vaughan-Lee, *The Circle of Love* (The Golden Sufi Center, 1999), ix.

9. Thich Nhat Hanh, *Love Letter to the Earth* (Parallax Press, 2013), 103.

10. The Haudenosaunee Confederacy, meaning "People of the Long-house," is one of the oldest-known participatory democracies in the world. It was originally composed of the Mohawk, Oneida, Onondaga, Cayuga, and Seneca nations, and later joined by the Tuscarora. Its governance blends law, values, and reverence for nature and the creator for their sustenance and well-being. Seventh-generational thinking arises from this tradition, reflecting a deep ethic of intergenerational responsibility.

11. Quoted by Anne-Marie Schimmel, *Mystical Dimensions of Islam* (University of North Carolina Press, 1975), 46.

12. Jalāl al-Dīn Muḥammad Rūmī, "Only Breath," in *The Essential Rumi*, trans. Coleman Barks (Harper Collins, 1996), 32.

13. Baha ad-din Naqshband, from the first of the eleven Naqshbandi principles. "The Eleven Principles of the Naqshbandi Path," Golden Sufi Center, accessed October 27, 2025. https://www.goldensufi .org/about/the-eleven-principles-of-the-naqshbandi-path.

14. Ruzbihan Baqli, *The Unveiling of Secrets: Diary of a Sufi Master,* trans. Carl W. Ernst (Parvardigar Press, 1997), 43.

15. Louis Massignon, *The Passion of al-Hallaj* (Princeton University Press, 1982), 285.

16. Ibn 'Arabi, *Fusus al-hikam* (Litera Yaylinari, 2016), 102.

17. Jake Skeets, "My Name Is Beauty," *Emergence Magazine, Volume 3: Living with the Unknown*, August 31, 2022, 157.

18. Paul Salopek, "A Path Older Than Memory," *Emergence Magazine, Volume 5: Time,* May 5 2024, 167.

19. Jalāl al-Dīn Muḥammad Rūmī, *Ripened Fruit, Love's Ripening: Rumi on the Heart's Journey*, trans. Kabir Helminski and Ahmad Rezwani (Shambhala Publications, 2008), 1.

20. Tyson Yunkaporta, "The Time Traveler's Wife's Husband," *Emergence Magazine, Volume 5: Time*, May 5, 2024, 231.

21. Persian song quoted by Irina Tweedie, *Daughter of Fire* (The Golden Sufi Center, 1986), 77.

22. Quoted by Claude Addas, *Quest for the Red Sulphur: The Life of Ibn 'Arabī*, trans. from the French by Peter Kingsley (The Islamic Texts Society, 1993), 61.

PERMISSIONS

Excerpt from "The First Water is the Body" from *Postcolonial Love Poem* by Natalie Dias, copyright © 2020 by Natalie Diaz. Reprinted with the permission of The Permissions Company, LLC on behalf of Graywolf Press, graywolfpress.org. Reprinted with the permission of Faber and Faber Ltd.

"When the Truth has taken hold of a heart" from *The Passion of al-Hallaj* by Louis Massignon, copyright © 1983 by Louis Massignon. Reprinted with permission of Princeton University Press, permission conveyed through Copyright Clearance Center, Inc.

"In the Dark Times" from *Collected Poems of Bertolt Brecht*, originally published in German in 1939 as "Motto: In den finsteren Zeiten," by Bertolt Brecht, translated by Tom Kuhn and David Constantine, copyright © 1976, 1961 by Bertolt-Brecht-Erben / Suhrkamp Verlag. Reprinted with the permission of Liveright Publishing Corporation.

Excerpts from *Love Letter to the Earth* by Thich Nhat Hanh, copyright © 2013 by Unified Buddhist Church, Inc., Plum Village Community

ABOUT THE AUTHOR

Emmanuel Vaughan-Lee is a Sufi teacher in the Naqshban-diyya-Mujaddidiyya tradition. He is the founder, podcast host, and executive editor of *Emergence Magazine*, a Webby Award-winning and National Magazine Award-nominated publication exploring the intersections of ecology, culture, and spirituality. An Emmy- and Peabody-nominated film-maker, he has directed over twenty documentary films, including *Taste of the Land*, *The Last Ice Age*, *Aloha ʻĀina*, *The Nightingale's Song*, *Earthrise*, *Sanctuaries of Silence*, and *Elemental*. His films have been screened at leading festivals such as the New York Film Festival, Tribeca, SXSW, and Hot Docs; exhibited at the Smithsonian and the Barbican; and featured by PBS, *National Geographic*, the *New York Times*, the *New Yorker*, and the *Atlantic*. Prior to his work in film and media, he performed with renowned jazz artists, releasing two acclaimed records—*Previous Misconceptions* and *Borrowed Time*. Emmanuel Vaughan-Lee leads retreats on Sufism and spiritual ecology worldwide. His work invites a deeper relationship with the living world through story, practice, and devotion.